How to Enjoy
Jesus

Printed in the United States of America

ISBN 1-933641-22-3

How to Enjoy
Jesus

Carroll Roberson

"... the **joy** of the Lord is your strength."

—Nehemiah 8:10

"... enter thou into the **joy** of thy lord."

—Matthew 25:21

Contents

Introduction

Being raised in rural Mississippi, where my father and mother came from extreme poverty, lack of education, where they were deprived of love and victims of dysfunctional families, we were not taught how to really enjoy life. My father never made very much money, and my mother had to work every day to make ends meet. My brother and I knew that we were loved, but the way of expressing that love came hard for our parents.

After I became a Christian, they did not know how to accept what God was doing in my life. When I felt the call to go into the ministry, they were very skeptical and confused about my decision. For many years they were uneasy about coming to services where I might be preaching or singing. Maybe they felt conviction about not teaching us Christian values early on, or maybe they just were not where they needed to be spiritually to receive what God was wanting to give them.

Those first years of trying to serve Jesus were very difficult for me, because I knew there was much more to the Christian faith than I was enjoying. Most of the church folks looked so sad, and you can tell by their expressions that they did not understand what it was like to be filled with God's Spirit, attending church was just a tradition, and they were in religious bondage, much like the people were in Jesus' time who lived under the Jewish leaders of Israel long ago.

I found myself caught in a trap, struggling to preach another sermon, trying to meet the expectations of the people, and trying to be accepted within the church system that man had created. There was no real joy there, no genuine peace, just following after everybody else. Most of the preachers I knew were in the same boat, but they did not know what to do either. As I traveled from place to place in evangelism, I saw that most professing Christians were just listening to their own denominational teachings, and were never looking for God in other people's lives, or outside of their own way of thinking. There was no one I could turn to, so I just started seeking myself for more truth to find the answer to why there was no real joy in my Christian life.

I started leading tours to Israel in the early nineties, and this was a step in the right direction, because no one had ever taught me how to really study the Scriptures. Realizing that Jesus was a Jew, and that He spoke Hebrew, really stirred my interest to dive deeper. I began to uncover the Jewish roots of the Christian faith, not Judaism, but the real faith of the Bible. The more I studied, the more I wanted to study. The more I learned about Jesus, the more I wanted to learn. God began to fill me with excitement about spiritual things, and He began to fill me with tremendous joy about His kingdom. After years of study, numerous trips to the Holy Land, living each day with a new perspective, my life has been changed. This work is a result of what I have experienced for myself. I have come to the place in my ministry that I do not want to give people just another sermon, or give them just another song, I want to share with them something that will help them live today for Christ, and help them to enjoy Him. I have lived what you are about to read, and even though I certainly have not arrived in my walk with Jesus, I never dreamed that it could be so real and so far above this present world.

My earthly father went to be with Jesus this year, and even though I miss him dearly, I know that it was the greatest day of his life when he was delivered from his pain-stricken body, and life of hardships. My mother continues on, working hard, and with the Lord's help she is doing well. I have seen the Lord bring her to another level in her life and it does my heart good. I don't think she fully understands the call that God has placed on my life, but I'm not sure I do either. I'm just trying to enjoy the ride. I trust that you will find how to really enjoy Jesus, because if you do, then others will want what you have, and that is what God intended from the very beginning.

If you do not know the Lord, my prayer is that the Holy Spirit will draw you when you search these pages, and you will come to know the joy of being a child of God. If you are a Christian, and you have lost your joy, may God do for you what He did for David many years ago, when David prayed:

Restore unto me the joy of thy salvation . . .

—Psalm 51:12a

The God of Blessing

God's original intent for all of creation was blessing. God blessed Adam and Eve, and even after they sinned, He still blessed them. Even though sin had come into the world through man's rebellion, God promised blessing to everyone who would believe in Him and follow Him. Many people think that God is a distant and harsh being who is just waiting to punish and judge human beings, and therefore they live in fear. But listen to some of these verses:

> The Lord is gracious, and full of compassion; slow to anger, and of great mercy. The Lord is good to all: and his tender mercies are over all his works.
>
> —Psalm 145:8–9

> For the Lord is good; his mercy is everlasting; and his truth endureth to all generations.
>
> —Psalm 100:5

> Fear not, little flock; for it is your Father's good pleasure to give you the kingdom.
>
> —Luke 12:32

He that loveth not knoweth not God; for God is love.

—1 John 4:8

Do these verses sound like God's intent is to punish people? Of course not! The Creator of the universe, who designed the earth, is a God of blessing. Even after man has proven that he was not interested in God for the most part, God still sent His Son to pay for the sin of the entire human race.

For God so loved the world, that he gave his only begotten Son, that whosoever believeth in him should not perish, but have everlasting life. For God sent not his Son into the world to condemn the world; but that the world through him might be saved.

—John 3:16–17

Blessed be the God and Father of our Lord Jesus Christ, who hath blessed us with all spiritual blessings in heavenly places in Christ.

—Ephesians 1:3

Even people who are not Christians enjoy God's blessings every day and do not realize it. The man who is not a believer may harvest a good crop as well as the saved man. Jesus talked about God's blessings this way: ". . . for he maketh his sun to rise on the evil and on the good, and sendeth rain on the just and on the unjust" (Matt. 5:45b).

When Christianity emerged from the Israelite community, the biblical practice of blessing was soon lost. The Greco–Roman world had virtually no tradition of blessing, and all they heard were prayers and benedictions from temple priests and religious leaders. Instead of going back to their Jewish roots, the new converts to Christianity just adapted to their own culture and surroundings. Soon the biblical emphasis on blessing was replaced by the institutional church system. The blessings of community were broken down, and were replaced by formal worship and led by professional clergy. We in the western world are victims of our own culture, and have been robbed of the richness of our biblical heritage. In a world that is filled with brokenness and loneliness, people desperately need to know that the God of the Bible is a God of blessing.

The most famous blessing in the mind of a religious Jew is: "The Lord bless thee, and keep thee: The Lord make his face shine upon thee, and be gracious unto thee: The Lord lift up his countenance upon thee, and give thee peace" (Num. 6:24–26).

Not only did God speak this blessing, but it was to be spoken over the Israelite community. To go even farther, listen to the next verse: "And they shall put my name upon the children of Israel; and I will bless them" (Num. 6:27).

By speaking this Aaronic blessing on the people, God's own personal name would be placed on them, and they would be blessed. This was not just a ceremony or a ritual, this was a powerful promise from God. We have severed ourselves so much from our Hebrew heritage that we have no concept of the real faith of Jesus and His apostles.

God made a covenant with a man named Abram, and later when God breathed on him and blessed him, his name was changed to AbraHam, and had the sound of God's name in his name, "Yahweh." That promise is recorded as follows:

> And I will make of thee a great nation, and I will bless thee, and make thy name great; and thou shalt be a blessing: And I will bless them that bless thee, and curse him that curseth thee: and in thee shall all families of the earth be blessed.
>
> —Genesis 12:2–3

God's blessing was first given to Abraham, his children, and then to the rest of the world. As this promise plays out in the New Testament, we see that everyone, Jew and Gentile, who believe like Abraham did, and trust in the Messiah Jesus, are also a part of this blessing.

> Even as Abraham believed God, and it was accounted to him for righteousness. Know ye therefore that they which are of faith, the same are the children of Abraham. And the scripture, foreseeing that God would justify the heathen through faith, preached before the gospel unto Abraham, saying, In thee shall all nations be blessed. So then they which be of faith are blessed with faithful Abraham.
>
> —Galatians 3:6–9

Through the death of Christ on the cross the blessing of Abraham has come to all who will believe, even Gentiles. If you are a believer in Christ, the Son of God, did you know that you are a child of Abraham, and you are part of that promise that God made to Abraham centuries ago? God has promised to bless us, and in return, we bless God, and those around us.

The Israelites knew that their blessings came from God, and this is why David wrote: "I will bless the Lord at all times: his praise shall continually be in my mouth" (Ps. 34:1).

God is so filled with goodness that he even works through the bad and the good in our lives. Sometimes we make bad choices, just like David made, sometimes other people do things against us, but through drawing close to God through faith in His Son Jesus, we can find forgiveness and God takes something bad and turns it into a blessing. Countless testimonies have been given over the years where people went through hardships, even disasters, and through it all God drew them to Himself, and turned it into something wonderful. The apostle Paul was a man who persecuted the Christians, and God called him to take the gospel to the Gentiles. Sometimes he went through suffering, sometimes he was rejected, and finally was beheaded at the hands of Nero, the Roman emperor. But listen to what he said just a short while before he died: "And we know that all things work together for good to them that love God, to them who are the called according to his purpose" (Rom. 8:28).

Why is this? Because God loves us so much, that He wants the very best for us, and He knows what brings peace and purpose to our lives. We go down many roads in our lives, and sometimes we have to reap what we sow in the flesh, but God is willing to forgive us and bless us in spite of it all.

So once we know that God is a God of blessing, then we want to bless Him, and bless those around us, yes, even our enemies.

> Ye have heard that it hath been said, Thou shalt love thy neighbor, and hate thine enemy. But I say unto you, Love your enemies, bless them that curse you, do good to them that hate you, and pray for them which despitefully use you, and persecute you.
>
> —Matthew 5:44

How can we not love others after God has shown such love to us? How could I hold a grudge against someone else, after God has forgiven me for all of the many failures in my own life? God has blessed me far beyond anything I could have ever dreamed of, and it is my turn to bless those around me. Before we can start to enjoy the salvation that God has extended to us, we have to know the character of the God who gave it to us. Sometimes I think that we preachers have done a lot of damage to the body of Christ over the years, by misrepresenting the God of the Bible. Some people see God as this screaming, yelling, forceful dictator, who wants to rob us of all of our joy in life. Because of certain styles and personalities, a lot of people have been turned off, and some of them may be lost forever. We must seek the heart of God, and quit listening to every church leader that comes along.

I used to feel so down and out, no confidence in the Lord or myself. I used to think that I had to live up to other people's opinions of me, until I found out that God loves me, and He has a plan for my life, and all of my sins are under the blood of His Son. Satan was robbing me of my blessing, through listening to ignorant people. It changed the course of my life, and when you realize how much God wants to bless you, it will change your life as well.

Thou art worthy, O Lord, to receive glory and honour and power: for thou hast created all things, and for thy pleasure they are and were created.

—Revelation 4:11

Baruch Ha Shem Adonai,
Blessed by the name of the Lord!

Jesus, a Man of Joy

One of the messianic prophecies calls Him, "a man of sorrows" (Isa. 53:3), and this is referring to the suffering servant phase of the Messiah. While it is true that Jesus of Nazareth suffered more than any man, and while He was a man of sorrows on the outside facing His death in Jerusalem, He was a man of joy on the inside.

Early on in the gospel narratives we see that joy would accompany the coming Messiah. When Mary came down to the hill country in Judæa and greeted Elizabeth, John the Baptist leaped in her womb for joy (Luke 1:44). When the angel of the Lord spoke to the shepherds who were abiding in the field at Bethlehem, the angel said, "Fear not: for, behold, I bring you good tidings of great joy, which shall be to all people. For unto you is born this day in the city of David a Saviour, which is Christ the Lord" (Luke 2:10–11).

When the wise men came to worship the Christ child, they saw the star that had went before them, and it stood over Jesus. "When they saw the star, they rejoiced with exceeding great joy" (Matt. 2:10).

The Messiah would bring joy not only to the wise men,

but to everyone who believed in Him. And this Messiah would also be filled with joy as He grew up in Nazareth, and as He started His earthly ministry in Galilee.

One of the things that always touches me when we take our yearly tours to Israel is that you find yourself in a strange paradox. Knowing that God walked where you are walking in the man Christ Jesus, and at the same time you feel the wind blow, you smell the flowers, you see the fish in the Sea of Galilee, and hear the laughter of the pilgrims, and when we get hungry we go and eat. The everyday circumstances that we all experience every day of our lives, Jesus, the Man of joy experienced.

Over the centuries most of the pictorial representations of Jesus show Him looking sad, mournful, and even weeping, which is certainly true. But there was another side to Jesus that we need to see, and it should not be offensive to anyone. Religion and church tradition has a way of blinding us from the real Jesus most of the time. But the common people in Galilee saw the real Messiah, and that is why they were attracted to Him. He showed them compassion, and they saw a joy about Him that they were not seeing in the religious people.

Try to imagine how Jesus of Nazareth grew up in a little, poor village as a carpenter's son. He grew up working hard, knowing how it feels to enjoy a good night's sleep, getting up and enjoying the sunrise, and enjoying the fruit of his labor. No doubt Jesus enjoyed working with Joseph, and seeing his mother prepare them a meal. Sometimes we forget that although Jesus was God, He was also Man, two distinct natures. We must keep in mind who Jesus is: "All things were made by him; and without him was not any thing made that was made. . . . He was in the world, and the world was made by him, and the world knew him not" (John 1:3, 10).

But at the same time we read: "And he was in the hinder part of the ship, asleep on a pillow . . ." (Mark 4:38a).

Or we find in another place these words:

"At that time Jesus went on the sabbath day through the corn; and his disciples were an hungred, and began to pluck the ears of corn, and to eat" (Matt. 12:1).

Jesus created the universe, but humbled Himself, and became a man.

> But made himself of no reputation, and took upon him the form of a servant, and was made in the likeness of men: And being found in fashion as a man, he humbled himself, and became obedient unto death, even the death of the cross.
>
> —Philippians 2:7–8

Can't you just see Jesus enjoying the wind. He talked about the salvation experience and used the March wind to describe it to Nicodemus. "The wind bloweth where it listeth, and thou hearest the sound thereof, but canst not tell whence it cometh, and whither it goeth: so is every one that is born of the Spirit" (John 3:8).

When Jesus was preaching the Sermon on the Mount at Galilee, He used the birds of the air when teaching his followers about worrying over the necessary things of life. "Behold the fowls of the air: for they sow not, neither do they reap, nor gather into barns; yet your heavenly Father feedeth them. Are ye not much better than they?" (Matt. 6:26).

One of the styles of teachings used by the rabbis in Jesus' day was called, *kalvyhomer,* which compared the big with the small. Jesus was using that style of teaching here saying that if the Father feeds the birds of the air, how much more will He feed you? Try to imagine how Jesus observed the birds of the air, and in Galilee you can hear them singing everywhere.

Jesus must have loved the flowers, because he said in the same sermon, "And why take ye thought for raiment? Consider the lilies of the field, how they grow; they toil not, neither do they spin: And yet I say unto you, That even Solomon in all his glory was not arrayed like one of these" (Matt. 6:28–29).

Jesus enjoyed the flowers, He put them there for our enjoyment, and to show us that He will take care of us.

When Jesus talked about the poor in spirit, those who mourn, the meek, those who hunger and thirst after righteousness, the merciful, the pure in heart, the peacemakers, and those who are persecuted for righteousness sake, He said they were, "Blessed." Not only will they be blessed in the future, they are blessed now! More fortunate than the rest of the world. Certainly "happy" does not mean the same thing as "blessed." People can be happy when their earthly circumstances are good, and still be spiritually lost, but when a person is blessed, they have God's favor in spite of their circumstances.

When teaching the disciples that one day they would become great fishers of men, Jesus performed a miracle of the draught of fishes, and the meaning was: "Fear not; from henceforth thou shalt catch men . . ." (Luke 5:10b).

The joy that Jesus must have had when He saw the eyes of those disciples when they drew in that great multitude of fishes. Jesus knew every fish in the Sea of Galilee, and He put them there for the people to enjoy. Can't you just see Jesus watching others enjoy the fishing business in those days.

One of the most powerful sermons Jesus ever gave was the parable of the sower in Matthew 13:1–9. Jesus must have had tremendous joy in His heart when He saw the farmers plowing their fields, planting the seed, and seeing them enjoy the harvest. Jesus designed the earth to bring forth food for us to eat.

Why the first miracle that Jesus performed was at a wedding feast, and they lasted for a week in those days. Many of the messages that Jesus gave in the gospels, He used a Jewish wedding as the backdrop, such as:

In my Father's house are many mansions, if it were not so I would have told you. I go to prepare a place for you and if I go to prepare a place for you, I will come again, and receive you unto myself; that where I am, there ye may be also.

—John 14:2–3

A Jewish man would propose to his bride, offer her a cup of wine, and if she accepted, he would go back to his father's house and build a room onto it for he and his bride. Her job was to keep an olive oil lamp in the window trimmed and burning. When the room was ready, he would go out into the night and get his bride, and there would be a big celebration with dancing and music. Jesus believed that what was good and beautiful in this world was to be enjoyed by human beings without apology.

Think of Jesus seeing the smiles and hearing the little children play. He used the children to give His disciples a great lesson on humility.

At the same time came the disciples unto Jesus, saying, Who is the greatest in the kingdom of heaven? And Jesus called a little child unto him, and set him in the midst of them, And said, Verily I say unto you, Except ye be converted, and become as little children, ye shall not enter into the kingdom of heaven. Whosoever therefore shall humble himself as this little child, the same is the greatest in the kingdom of heaven.

—Matthew 18:1–4

In the time of Jesus the fathers would lay their hands on

their children and bless them. Jesus blessed the little children, and can't you just see the joy illuminating from His face?

Jesus said when we are persecuted for our faith that we should, "Rejoice in that day, and leap for joy . . ." (Luke 6:23a). He said that we should not be like the Pharisees of His day, we should rejoice when a sinner is saved. "I say unto you, that likewise joy shall be in heaven over one sinner that repenteth, more than over ninety and nine just persons, which need no repentance" (Luke 15:7). One of the most familiar parables Jesus ever gave is the story of the prodigal son. After the son had went away with his inheritance, and wasted his money on wild living, he came to himself and went back home to his father. When the father saw his son coming from the distance, the father ran and embraced his son. And even though the son told his father he was not worthy to be called his son anymore, the father made the servants bring the best robe, put a ring on his hand, shoes on his feet, and kill the fatted calf. The words are written: ". . . And they began to be merry" (Luke 15:24b). The religious people of the day were murmuring because Jesus was taking up time with the publicans and sinners, and they should have been rejoicing. Many times we do not rejoice when we see someone who used to be very immoral or wayward come to Christ. We are so sinful that we still pass judgment on God's children, even though God has forgiven them. The Christian life is one of joy according to Jesus, especially when someone comes home to the Father!

Even though Jesus knew that His time on earth would be short, and that He must face the cross in Jerusalem, listen to what the scriptures say: "Looking unto Jesus the author and finisher of our faith; who for the joy that was set before him endured the cross, despising the shame, and is set down at the right hand of the throne of God" (Heb. 12:2). How could there be joy in the heart of Jesus, knowing He was going to a cross to be crucified? Because He was going to conquer death and rise again! He was going to prepare a way for us to be with Him in Heaven someday. So now if we follow Christ, we can even have joy in death. The test of our faith is during the time of death. Are we afraid to die? It's normal to weep when our loved ones leave us, but do we find joy in the promises of the Lord? We normally have it backward, and we rejoice when a baby is born and weep when someone dies. But the Bible says: "Precious in the sight of the Lord, is the death of his saints" (Ps. 116:15).

After Jesus died on the cross, the disciples were filled with dismay and sadness. The One who had given them a new beginning in life was crucified by the Romans, rejected by the nation of Israel. What were they to do? They had left their occupations, and had walked the dusty roads of Israel with their Lord, and now He was gone. Then we read in John 20:19–20,

Then the same day at evening, being the first day of the week, when the doors were shut where the disciples were assembled for fear of the Jews, came Jesus and stood in the midst, and saith unto them, Peace be unto you. And when he had so said, he showed them his hands and his side. Then were the disciples glad, when they saw the Lord.

The resurrection of the Messiah brought such joy to the disciples that they would never turn back from following Christ, not even when death came, because they had seen the risen Lord!

One of the moments in the earthly ministry of Jesus that is so overlooked, is His ascension. Listen to what happened:

> And he led them out as far as to Bethany, and he lifted up his hands, and blessed them. And it came to pass, while he blessed them, he was parted from them, and carried up into heaven. And they worshiped him, and returned to Jerusalem with great joy: And were continually in the temple, praising and blessing God. Amen.
>
> —Luke 24:50–53

They were not sad, they were not gloomy, they returned with great joy! Even the going away back to Heaven was a time of joy for the disciples. I've had the privilege to stand on the Mount of Olives many times, the place where Jesus ascended from, and let me tell you, you can still feel the joy that Jesus left behind, if you know Him as your personal Savior.

We are to delight ourselves in the Lord. Even though our lives are filled sometimes with dark moments, like the life of Jesus was, this world cannot take away our joy. Jesus knew the end of the story would be wonderful, and we are supposed to focus on what God has waiting for us in the end. Because sin came into the world, there is tribulation, but what did Jesus say? ". . . In the world ye shall have tribulation: but be of good cheer, I have overcome the world" (John 16:33b). This is the thing that is missing in most Christians lives. Jesus has to be our focus, and when He is where he needs to be in our lives, we will be filled with joy!

Jesus had a mission to accomplish, and He did it with joy. He enjoyed His eternal life that He had with the Father, and that is what we are supposed to be doing. No wonder the people were coming from everywhere to see and to hear this man called Jesus. The hills and mountains of Galilee were crowded with multitudes of people from Syria, Tyre and Sidon, Samaria, Judæa, Perea, Jerusalem, Galilee, the Decapolis, and why? It was a dark moment in the history of mankind, and the Light had come, Jesus, the Man of joy! *Todah Lechah Yeshua,* Thank you Jesus! *Anee Ohev Otchah Yeshua,* I love you Jesus!

So what is God's ultimate purpose? "For God so loved the world, that he gave his only begotten Son, that whosoever believeth in him should not perish, but have everlasting life. For God sent not his Son into the world to condemn the world; but that the world through him might be saved" (John 3:16–17). Does that sound like something to be sad about? It's all about believing in Jesus, God's Son, and when we do, we are not condemned, but we have everlasting life!

The Holy Spirit

The blessed Holy Spirit was there when everything was created in the beginning. ". . . And the Spirit of God moved [*rachaph*] upon the face of the waters" (Gen. 1:2b). The same wording is used when Jesus the Messiah was baptized. "And John bare record, saying, I saw the Spirit descending from heaven like a dove, and it abode upon him" (John 1:32). The picture is that the Spirit fluttered, or brooded over the waters, bringing about creation. When Jesus was baptized, the same Spirit brooded over Him bringing about a new creation.

Also, we find when the Spirit was working when man was created. "And God said, Let us make man in our image, after our likeness . . ." (Gen. 1:26a). The Father, the Son, and the Holy Spirit were involved in creating man. If anyone ever doubted the existence of God, all they have to do is look another human being. Just to see how we are created, walking upright, two legs, two arms, two hands, two eyes, being able to see, to hear, to smell, to taste, to feel, to choose for ourselves, proves the existence of God.

Through God sending His Son Jesus into the world,

through His death and resurrection, we can now enjoy life the way God intended, through the indwelling Holy Spirit. When a person is truly born again, they are born of the Spirit. "Jesus answered, Verily, verily, I say unto thee, Except a man be born of water and of the Spirit, he cannot enter into the kingdom of God. That which is born of the flesh is flesh; and that which is born of the Spirit is spirit" (John 3:5-6). Jesus talking to Nicodemus about the new birth, gives him the contrast between the physical and the spiritual birth.

The only way one can truly worship a Holy God, is to be filled with the Holy Spirit. "But the hour cometh, and now is, when the true worshiper shall worship the Father in spirit and in truth: for the Father seeketh such to worship him. God is a Spirit: and they that worship him must worship him in spirit and in truth" (John 4:23-24). God cannot be reached through the physical, just like the Samaritan woman came searching for physical water, but Jesus told her about the living water, that would truly satisfy the thirst of the soul. Once she tasted of the living water, she forgot all about the physical water, and found such joy, that she ran back to the city and told the people about Christ.

We cannot talk about joy, without referring to the Holy Spirit. "But the fruit of the Spirit is love, joy, peace, longsuffering, gentleness, goodness, faith, meekness, temperance: against such there is no law" (Gal. 5:22-23).

When Jesus was in the upper room in Jerusalem with His disciples, He told them:

And I will pray the Father, and he shall give you another
Comforter, that he may abide with you forever; Even the
Spirit of truth; whom the world cannot receive, because
it seeth him not, neither knoweth him: but ye know him;
for he dwelleth with you, and shall be in you.

—John 14:16–17

It is the Holy Spirit who gives us comfort when the storms
of life come our way. It is the Holy Spirit who guides us
into all truth, and who teaches us the Scriptures. "But the
Comforter, which is the Holy Ghost, whom the Father will
send in my name, he shall teach you all things, and bring all
things to your remembrance, whatsoever I have said unto
you" (John 14:26). We can go to church all of our lives, and
read the Bible for years and years, and never grasp the great
truths of God, and never have real assurance in our lives, if
we are not filled with the Holy Spirit.

As our Lord was walking with His disciples on the way
to the Garden of Gethsemane, He said: " These things have I
spoken unto you, that my joy might remain in you, and that
your joy might be full" (John 15:11). Through the indwelling Holy Spirit, we can have the joy of Jesus! The disciples
would be very sorrowful when they saw Jesus die on the
cross, but listen to what Jesus promised to them: "Verily,
verily, I say unto you, That ye shall weep, and lament, but
the world shall rejoice: and ye shall be sorrowful, but your
sorrow shall be turned to joy" (John 16:20). Joy is Hebrew
is *simchah,* "exceeding bliss," and these disciples would ex-

perience joy that the world could not understand when they saw the risen Lord. ". . . And your joy no man taketh from you" (John 16:22b). The world could not take away what it cannot give. Once these disciples received the real joy of the Spirit, they gave their lives for the cause of Christ, nothing could cause them to turn back.

The way we learn more about Jesus is through the help of the Holy Spirit. "But when the Comforter is come, whom I will send unto you from the Father, even the Spirit of truth, which proceedeth from the Father, he shall testify of me" (John 15:26). "He shall glorify me . . ." (John 16:14a). The work of the Holy Spirit is to show us Jesus, our need of Jesus, who He is, the work He has done, and the work He has for us to do in this life.

When the apostle Paul was talking in the fourteenth chapter of Romans, he said we should not judge our brothers about what they eat or do not eat, or what day they regard. Jewish Christians regarded the Sabbath day, while Gentile Christians regarded another day. Today we still have the same problem; there are those who act more spiritual because of what they do or do not eat, and what day they decided to worship on. But Paul went on to say, "For the kingdom of God is not meat and drink; but righteousness, peace, and joy in the Holy Ghost" (Rom. 14:17). We should never try to place brothers or sisters in bondage, by making them feel guilty about eating certain foods, and try to look more spiritual than someone else. The kingdom of God is not about legalism; it's about being filled with the joy of the

Holy Spirit. We should strive to edify the brethren instead of accusing them.

So the secret is to be filled with the Holy Spirit. It's not in what we do, or who we are; it's all about receiving the Holy Spirit into our lives. So many Christians in our world our afraid of the Holy Spirit. They have seen so much on Christian television that has confused them, and Satan has used this to keep many people from enjoying the Lord. Try getting up every morning and ask the Holy Spirit to fill you each day. Ask Him to teach you more about Jesus; ask Him to guide you; ask Him to give you the joy of Jesus. Before you study the Bible, ask Him to reveal God's truths to you; ask Him to pray for you; ask Him to teach you how to worship God.

If we feed the flesh in our lives more than we do the Spirit, then we are going to not only be very carnal people, but we will not have the joy the Bible talks about. If we live more for the Spirit, we can rise above our circumstances and our problems, and have joy no matter what comes our way. I see most believers today living such a sad life, spending all their time and money on the things that will pass away, while the Lord has a wonderful life for us to enjoy, with purpose and with excitement about His kingdom.

But we must commit our lives to the things that will count in eternity. Not only is it for our personal joy, but also for the people around us, to see the joy of the Lord in our lives.

The Holy Spirit in Hebrew is *Ruach Haqodesh,* and the

word, *ruach* means "wind" or "breath." So when you feel the wind blowing, or when you breathe, be reminded of His presence in your life each day, and start living your life being filled with the joy of the Holy Spirit!

The Holy Scriptures

How sweet are thy words unto my taste! Yea, sweeter
than honey to my mouth!

—Psalm 119:103

In ancient Bible days, while teaching the young children the
Hebrew scriptures, they would use a small clay tablet. The
Hebrew scriptures would be written with a sharpened reed
on the clay tablet, and then they would spread honey over
the tablet. When the children took their reeds and tried to
find what the scriptures were that the rabbis had written
down, they would have to make their way through the honey, and in so doing, they would lick the honey from the reed
as they went along. This way, the rabbis were teaching them
that God's law was sweet, and this would go with them the
rest of their life. This may be where the idea of the psalmist
was taken from.

There are over five hundred references in the Bible to
joy, and over one hundred just in the Psalms alone. If you
just read Psalm 119, you will find many verses about the joy
of God's Word.

I will delight myself in thy statutes: I will not forget thy word.

—verse 16

Make me to go in the path of thy commandments; for therein do I delight.

—Verse 35

And I will delight myself in thy commandments, which I have loved.

—Verse 47

The law of thy mouth is better unto me than thousands of gold and silver.

—Verse 72

Let thy tender mercies come unto me, that I may live: for thy law is my delight.

—Verse 77

Unless thy law had been my delights, I should then have perished in mine affliction.

—Verse 92

O how I love thy law! It is my meditation all the day.

—Verse 97

Thy word is a lamp unto my feet, and a light unto my path.

—Verse 105

Thy testimonies have I taken as an heritage for ever: for they are the rejoicing of my heart.

—Verse 111

I hate vain thoughts: but thy law do I love.

—Verse 113

Therefore I love thy commandments above gold; yea, above fine gold.

—Verse 127

Thy word is very pure: therefore thy servant loveth it.

—Verse 140

Trouble and anguish have taken hold on me: yet thy commandments are my delights.

—Verse 143

Consider how I love thy precepts: quicken me, O Lord, according to thy lovingkindness.

—Verse 159

I rejoice at thy word, as one that findeth great spoil.

—Verse 162

Great peace have they which love thy law: and nothing shall offend them.

—Verse 165

> I have longed for thy salvation, O Lord; and thy law is my delight.
>
> —Verse 174

If the psalmist could love the Jewish law, how much more should we love the whole Word of the Lord? Now that the Messiah has come, and paid the price for the sins of the world, Jews and Gentiles, we should delight in the words of Jesus, who came to set us free from the penalty of the law that we could not keep. "All scripture is given by inspiration of God, and is profitable for doctrine, for reproof, for correction, for instruction in righteousness" (2 Tim. 3:16).

There is joy in studying the Holy Scriptures! The Scriptures have meant so much to me over the years. Sometimes they correct me and I feel convicted. Sometimes they show me where I have misunderstood what the Bible was saying. Sometimes I realize how little I know about the Bible, but the Scriptures always bring joy to my life, because I know that God loves me, and He desires the best for me.

As I have talked to hundreds of people over the years, the number one problem seems to be that most people doubt the truths of the Scriptures. They may never say anything to anyone about it, but they question God's Word. We live in a world where people are very intelligent, and they are smart at business, good with computers, educated in world travel, and they have a problem when it comes to the validity of the Scriptures. But I tell them the Scriptures are more true than our logic. There are things in the Bible that I do not understand, and sometimes I may wonder why God allowed certain things to happen, but I have no doubt that the Bible is the Word of God! Science has proven it to be true over and over again. History and archaeology have proven it to be true. Millions of people over the centuries have found solace and comfort in God's holy Word. But the most compelling evidence is a changed life, and I can tell you firsthand that the Lord Jesus Christ has changed my life, and His Word has brought great joy to my heart.

We must learn how to enjoy Jesus through studying the sacred Scriptures. One of the reasons why so many professing believers do not find joy in the Scriptures, is because they have never learned how to study the Bible. The average Christian just gets a little truth here and there, and they never find the hidden treasures of the Bible. Once you learn how to study the Bible, and how to approach God's Word, then you will look forward to spending time in the Scriptures.

Learn how to keep the Scriptures in their proper context, and watch out for denominational interpretations. Who is doing the talking? Who are they talking to? What is the situation spiritually, politically, and geographically? Then, what is the lesson that God is trying to teach you through that scripture? One of the things that hurts me deeply is to hear someone take a passage of scripture completely out of context in order get people to believe what they are trying to say. Don't over–spiritualize the Scriptures, just glean from them what the main truth is. Get a good study Bible, and watch how the old scriptures are fulfilled in the Messiah. Run down your reference verses, and also do word studies from a *Strong's Concordance.*

Because the language of the Scriptures was originally Hebrew in the Old Testament, and we know that the primary language of Jesus was Hebrew, it really brings more light to the verses when you trace down the verses in Hebrew. Even though the New Testament was written in Greek, the proper way to study is from the Hebrew. Greek was the intermediate language of the Roman Empire. The gospel of Matthew was written in Hebrew first, and even the writings of Paul have a Hebrew background to them. There are many study helps you can find, such as an interlinear Bible, that will help you to dig a little deeper in the Word. Learn the manners and customs of the Bible so you can place yourself in the proper setting.

I am convinced that the only true way to study the Scriptures is from the Jewish perspective. Not Judaism, but the true Jewish faith of Abraham, the prophets, and the faith of Jesus. Let me give you a few examples of what I mean:

1. **Jesus was a Jew**—John 4:9
2. **Salvation was to the Jew first**—John 4:22; Romans 1:16
3. **Jesus read the Hebrew Scriptures**—Luke 24:27,44
4. **Jesus spoke Hebrew primarily**—Acts 26:14
5. **Blindness in part has happened to Israel**—Romans 11:25

6. **Even believing Gentiles are children of Abraham**—Galatians 3:6–9, 13–14

God is not through with the Jewish people; some verses pertain to the unbelieving Jews, and some pertain to the church—Jew and Gentile believers. Don't ever try to take out Israel, and replace them with the church. This teaching has caused tremendous chaos in the church over the centuries. I'm afraid the Gentiles have tried to invent their own Christianity over the years, without knowing their Jewish roots. I say all of that to help you better understand the Scriptures so you can find joy when you study.

We know that Jesus is the Messiah, the Son of God according to the Scriptures.

> And many other signs truly did Jesus in the presence of his disciples, which are not written in this book: But these are written, that ye might believe that Jesus is the Christ, the Son of God; and that believing ye might have life through his name.
>
> —John 20:30–31

We know that He died and rose again, according to the Scriptures.

> For I delivered unto you first of all that which I also received, how that Christ died for our sins according to

the scriptures; And that he was buried, and that he rose again the third day according to the scriptures.

—1 Corinthians 15:3–4

Enjoying Jesus really reaches a mountain top when the written Word, becomes the living Word in your life! Don't settle for *status quo* Christianity, there is so much joy hidden in the Holy Scriptures!

Keeping Our Focus on God's Kingdom

One of the big problems we have as believers, especially in the Western world, is keeping our focus on God's kingdom, and this in return robs us of the joy that God has for us. The Hebrew word for kingdom is *malkuw,* which means "dominion" or "reign." So the kingdom of God is when God has dominion in our lives, or He reigns on the throne of our hearts. When reading in the gospel accounts, sometimes it is also referred to as, the kingdom of Heaven, which is a Jewish synonym for God.

For example, when Jesus came into Galilee preaching "the kingdom of God is at hand," He was offering people a glorious alternative to what they had. Most of the people in Galilee were ruled by the oppression of the Romans, heavy taxation, and Jesus was offering them Himself. In other words, you may live under earthly Roman earthly, but I will give you peace, love, and joy, and my kingdom is not of this world. Jesus came to be their focus, and if they would receive Him and His kingdom, then their attention would not be on the Romans any longer.

Most of the common people were under the religious oppression of the scribes and Pharisees in the time of Jesus, and they had no real hope to offer the people—just rules, traditions of men, and religious bondage. Jesus the Messiah came offering them His kingdom of truth, rest, hope, and something real from the Father in Heaven. To the people who were burdened down, Jesus said,

> Come unto me, all ye that labour and are heavy laden, and I will give you rest. Take my yoke upon you, and learn of me; for I am meek and lowly in heart: and ye shall find rest unto your souls. For my yoke is easy, and my burden is light.
>
> —Matthew 11:28–30

Jesus came offering them a kingdom that would lift their burdens, and His kingdom would not be a boring, dry, formal drudgery. Serving in His kingdom would be a delight, because Jesus was truly the King of the kingdom, and what He had to offer was not pretense, but the real peace they needed in their lives.

Again, in that great sermon that Jesus gave on the hillsides north of the Sea of Galilee, He said, " But seek ye first the kingdom of God, and his righteousness; and all these things shall be added unto you" (Matt. 6:33). What things? The everyday needs that we all have—food and clothing. So much of the time we spend more time on worrying about these things, instead of God's kingdom, that we spend our energy and money on the things that are going to vanish away, instead of the eternal kingdom of God. Jesus says if we will focus on His kingdom first, then He will provide those earthly needs we have. Do we really believe He will? We are talking about having joy in our lives, and the way to enjoy Jesus is to keep the main thing, the main thing. My time, my money, my talents, my motive, my ambition, my goal in life should be to promote God's kingdom. If I do that, then God will provide the physical things I need. He provided salvation for us through His Son; He can certainly take care of our earthly needs.

I've never been able to understand why most professing believers concentrate on trying to have so much wealth, such as nice homes, cars, bank accounts, and all the trinkets they desire, when Jesus plainly told us: "And again I say unto you, It is easier for a camel to go through the eye of a needle, than for a rich man to enter into the kingdom of God" (Matt. 19:24). One of the ways to get people's attention in those days, was by using "hyperboles," an extreme situation. Jesus was talking about a real needle, and a real camel to stir their minds and hearts. Today, we try to explain all of that away because we are living in a materialistic society where people do not want to accept the true teachings of Jesus.

In that wonderful chapter where Jesus talked about the mysteries of the kingdom of Heaven, He gave the parable of the hidden treasure. "Again, the kingdom of heaven is like unto treasure hid in a field; the which when a man hath found, he hideth, and for joy thereof goeth and selleth all that he hath, and buyeth that field" (Matt. 13:44). The problem with most people, the devil has blinded their minds from the kingdom of God. They have never seen it, and they do not know what a treasure it is. Once we see God's kingdom—that we can be a part of it, and serve in it—then we will give up everything else just to be included. And we will do it with joy!

I talk to so many ministers who are discouraged, and many church members who are downtrodden. When we focus on our church, or our ministry, instead of God's kingdom, then we will sooner or later get discouraged. It's not about me, or you, or my church, or your church, it's about God's kingdom. People will wear you down; religious systems will wear you down; but God will fill you with joy. So sad that the only kingdom some people ever see is their little kingdom, and they want everybody else to fit into their ideas. Many churches exclude the poor, the outcast, the ones who really need to hear the message of Christ because they want their church to fit into the modern-day world. We can promote ourselves and say we are doing God's work, but God knows those who are pure in heart, and He is looking at our motives. We can see something that may look big in our eyes, but God sees the heart. ". . . For that which is highly esteemed among men is abomination in the sight of God" (Luke 16:15b). There are many self-made prophets in the world who rake in millions of dollars each year, but God is keeping a record, and one day He will judge the secrets of all men.

We have to realize that life is a gift from God, and that gift is for Him. When life is given back to God, then He fills us with the joy that He intended for us to have. It is a narrow way, and to be filled with joy, our focus must be on God's kingdom.

One day our physical lives will deteriorate, and we will have a Christian funeral, with flowers, music, and a crowd of people. The minister may say a lot of good things about us, some may weep, and we may even have a nice tombstone placed on our grave. But life will go on, and we will soon be forgotten, like a rock thrown into a river, we make a little splash, and then the river flows on. So knowing that to be true, why not focus our lives on something that will count in eternity? It's not going to matter one day how many cows we had, or how big our house was, or how much money we made, or even how long we lived on earth. It's not even going to matter how many children we had, and how good our reputation was. All that will matter is, did we accept Christ, did we serve Christ to the best of our ability? What was number one in our lives? If it was God's kingdom, and helping others get into His kingdom, and promoting the work of the Lord around the world, wanting others to meet this Jesus who changed our life, then it will not matter if we even have a funeral, for we will be with our Lord, and we will see Him face to face!

Over the years I have found so much joy in serving

Christ, that I will never be the same, and the things of this world seem to be so temporary. You want to enjoy Jesus, keep your focus on His kingdom, and **beware** of the kingdoms of this world.

Enjoy Jesus in the Mystery

One of the most important ways to enjoy Jesus is to keep the mystery alive, and do not try to always understand the ways of God. We live in a modern–day, high technological world, where man has invented the television, the radio, the telephone, jet airplanes, computers, skyscraper buildings, and that is using simple words to describe a very complicated world. The danger bleeds over into our spiritual lives sometimes, and we think we are supposed to understand everything about God, and about the Bible. Many have tried, and they always come up more confused than when they started. That is because our human minds cannot comprehend the mind of God. I have read where many scientists, who once were atheists, have come to believe in Jesus as their personal Savior, because the more they studied science, the more they found the Bible to be true. Let me give you a few scriptures to show you my point.

For my thoughts are not your thoughts, neither are your ways my ways, saith the Lord. For as the heavens are higher than the earth, so are my ways higher than your ways, and my thoughts than your thoughts.

—Isaiah 55:8–9

Who hath measured the waters in the hollow of his hand, and meted out heaven with the span, and comprehended the dust of the earth in a measure, and weighed the mountains in scales, and the hills in a balance? Who hath directed the Spirit of the Lord, or being his counsellor hath taught him?

—Isaiah 40:12–13

God gives us enough understanding to know that we need salvation, we can sense our sin and unworthiness. He gives us enough knowledge to take care of our families, and how to survive on the planet, but we can only go so far. And when we step into the eternal things, if we do not leave the mysteries to God, we will lose our joy.

Let me give you a case in point. Let's say that being a Christian only involves joining a local church, walking down the aisle, getting water baptized, trying to live the best you can, and reading your Bible as often as possible. If that was all there was to Christianity, then there is no mystery! We have taken the supernatural out of biblical Christianity today, and turned it into something we can do for ourselves, and therefore, it is only a system of religious mechanics. But that is not what the Scriptures say. Paul told the church at Ephesus to pray for him, so he could ". . . make known the mystery of the gospel" (Eph. 6:19b). The gospel of Jesus Christ itself is a mystery. How a person can trust in Jesus of Nazareth as the Son of God, who lived two thousand years ago, and died on a cross, and believe that God raised Him from the dead, and then they will be saved. How simple childlike faith reaches up to a powerful, eternal God, who created Heaven and earth. Jesus said salvation was like the wind—nobody can explain the wind, but you can feel it. When Jesus explained the kingdom in parables, He called His teachings "the mysteries of the kingdom of heaven." Unexplainable, but now we can see that Jesus' words came true.

When Paul wrote to the church at Colosse, he told them about another great mystery.

Even the mystery which hath been hid from ages and from generations, but now is made manifest to his saints: To whom God would make known what is the riches of the glory of this mystery among the Gentiles; which is Christ in you, the hope of glory.
—Colossians 1: 26–27

It was inconceivable for Gentiles to be included in God's kingdom to the religious Jews. But what is even a greater mystery, is that the Jewish Messiah, Yeshua, Jesus the Christ, will live inside of any Jew or Gentile who will come to Him by faith.

Who can explain such a mystery as this? You mean the

Son of God will live inside of me? Yes, indeed my friend, and He will give you overflowing joy, if you will walk by faith and not sight.

The fact that Jesus of Nazareth was man, yet He was God, is the greatest mystery of all. "And without controversy great is the mystery of godliness: God was manifest in the flesh, justified in the Spirit, seen of angels, preached unto the Gentiles, believed on in the world, received up into glory" (1 Tim. 3:16) Can you explain that one? Of course not! But Jesus proved that He was God by the works that He performed. No normal man ever walked on water, or calmed a raging storm, or open someone's eyes who had been born blind. No one ever died on a cross and walked out of the tomb to tell about it. He was a phenomenon!

I can't explain to anyone what happened to me when I surrendered my life to Christ. All I know is I have been different since that day. His joy is in my heart more today than any time in my life, and that is why I am writing to you now. Just like I can't explain a sunrise or a sunset, how the stars are all different from one another, or why the sky is blue, or why the oceans do not flood the land, or how the earth revolves around the sun in perfect order, and the exact distance away from the sun. I rejoice in the handiwork of God, and I rejoice in Christ my Savior, and I'm glad I cannot understand it, because if I could, then God would not be God.

So when you study the Bible, and you come across something you do not understand, just praise God, and leave that in God's hands. When something bad happens to good people, and when something good happens to bad people, don't worry about, God will level the playing ground one day soon. Enjoy Jesus, and enjoy the mystery!

Enjoy Jesus in Salvation

Behold, God is my salvation; I will trust, and not be afraid: for the Lord Jehovah is my strength and my song; he also is become my salvation. Therefore with joy shall ye draw water out of the wells of salvation.

—Isaiah 12:2–3

Salvation is totally a free gift from God; there is nothing we could ever do to deserve it or to earn it. How long has it been since you saw someone accept God's salvation with joy? There certainly must be remorse and repentance for our sins, but when we receive God's gift of eternal salvation, there should be joy in our hearts.

Over the years I have had the unique privilege of seeing countless people receive Christ as their Savior, and some of them expressed overflowing joy, sometimes with tears of joy, sometimes with a holy laughter. I think the reason so many do not respond in joy is because they do not understand what God has done for them. When I see the sad looks on people's faces in many of the churches where we go, I wonder if they have ever really experienced God's gift of salvation, or did they just join the local church. I want to give you the picture that God gives us in the Scriptures. There is our sin, and then there is God's wonderful gift through His Son, Jesus.

In the old covenant, there were six hundred thirteen laws, and it was impossible for man to keep the law perfectly, but it was a "schoolmaster to bring us to Christ" (Gal. 3:24). When we read the Scriptures we see our guilt—all of us have fallen short in more ways than we want to count. We are so sinful that not only do we have to deal with the sins of the flesh, but we have to fight the sins of the spirit as well, such as pride, jealousy, anger, unforgiveness, etc. To give you an example of how sinful we are, we can watch hours and hours of television movies, and we struggle to read one chapter in God's Word a day. We can read a novel for weeks which does not help our spiritual lives at all, but we can't even come to Bible study. We can spend thousands of dollars on ourselves trying to impress those around us, and we struggle to give a twenty dollar bill to support the Lord's work. We remember the bad things that someone does in their life, and we seldom ever spread the good things they have done. Even when we do something for the Lord, we sometimes want to be recognized, and a plaque placed in our honor for it. We are sometimes glad to hear about some Christian who has fallen, and we do nothing to lift them back up. We give our money to those who can give to us in return, instead of giving to those who cannot return the favor. We like to have over guests at our home who our respectable and upstanding citizens of the community, but we would never invite the poor and the welfare recipients of our town. And with all of the sin in our lives, and with all of the things we have failed to do that we should have done, "For scarcely for a righteous man will one die: yet peradventure for a good man some would even dare to die. But God commendeth his love toward us, in that, while we were yet sinners, Christ died for us" (Rom. 5:7–8)

You might find someone who would die for a righteous person, maybe, but God sent Christ to die for us sinners.

When Jesus was being criticized by the Pharisees for taking up time with the outcasts, Jesus said, "They that be whole need not a physician, but they that are sick. But go ye and learn what that meaneth, I will have mercy, and not sacrifice: for I am not come to call the righteous, but sinners to repentance" (Matt. 9:12–13). The ones who think they are okay spiritually do not feel their need of a Savior. And that's the problem with is—we measure ourselves among ourselves, and therefore we look okay compared to someone else. But when we compare ourselves beside a holy, eternal God, who is perfect in all His ways, we look as sinful as can be. But through sending Jesus into the world to die on the cross for us, who was a perfect sacrifice, now listen to what has happened: "To declare, I say, at this time his righteousness: that he might be just, and the justifier of him which believeth in Jesus" (Rom. 3:26). There was a holy justice that had to be satisfied. God, being holy, could not just look down and say, "I forgive you"; there had to be a price paid for sin to satisfy His justice. We cannot understand it because we do not know perfection. But the moment that we turn to the blood of Christ, we are counted righteous in God's eyes. "For he hath made him to be sin for us, who knew no sin; that we might be made the righteousness of God in him" (2 Cor. 5:21). Can you say, "Praise God"? Can you rejoice? Are you getting the picture?

Listen to how Paul describes the contrast between the old covenant and the new covenant:

> But if the ministration of death, written and engraven in stones, was glorious, so that the children of Israel could not steadfastly behold the face of Moses for the glory of his countenance, which glory was to be done away: How shall not the ministration of the spirit be rather glorious?
>
> —2 Corinthians 3:7–8

We are guilty under the old law, but we have been redeemed under the new. And one of the most dangerous things is when someone does not know the difference between law and grace, or they have been saved by grace, and are still trying to live under the law. Most churches today teach grace, but then they mix the law in with grace when teaching the Bible. For example: If you have accepted Jesus, are you still bound to the Jewish law of keeping the Sabbath? Are you still bound by the Jewish law of tithing? Are you still bound to the Old Testament sacrificial system? Do you still bring offerings to the temple in Jerusalem? Do you get the point? While there are principles laid down in the Old Testament that still apply today, we are not bound by the Jewish law. If someone wants to worship on Saturday, that is fine, or if someone wants to give a tenth to the church, that is fine, but they should not feel in bondage, or make others feel in bondage. The Messiah has come; He is our complete rest; He is the complete sacrifice; He fulfilled the law that no man could ever fulfill. Now, God does not live in a building, like the days of King Solomon, He does not live in a church building, but in the hearts of His children. If you do not rightly divide the Word of truth, you will be confused, and lose your joy. If we seek the face of Jesus in our salvation, then we will be changed by His glory (2 Cor. 3:18). That's why it is so important that we don't lose our focus, and enjoy Jesus in our salvation.

We have heard this old story so much in our culture that it has lost its meaning, and we have lost the excitement of being a child of God. We should be anxious to come to Christ. We should be excited about telling others what He has done for us. We should be overjoyed to get to read the Scriptures. We have been set free, we have been sanctified, we have been cleansed by the blood of Jesus!

Some people go to church and they go home the same way they came, empty. If you do not feel the Spirit of the Lord in your services, then you are just going through a traditional ritual called "church." There is supposed to be some joy in our salvation.

Not only has Christ forgiven us, He keeps on forgiving us. "If we confess our sins, he is faithful and just to forgive us our sins, and to cleanse us from all unrighteousness" (1 John 1:9). We don't have to walk around with the heavy guilt of yesterday's mistakes; the blood of Jesus makes us white as snow.

When I think back on my life—how lonely I was, and how I couldn't find purpose for my life, and how Christ has not only given my salvation, He has given me a life of purpose, and has called me into His ministry—sometimes when I'm driving down the road, I just have to shout and thank God for what He has done for me. "Thanks be unto God for his unspeakable gift" (2 Cor. 9:15).

One of the great Christians of years gone by was, John Newton, who had been a very open sinner working out on the sea in the 1800s. He later received Christ and wrote the song "Amazing Grace," which has probably been sung more than any spiritual song in our culture. But when he was getting on up in the years, his mind started failing him, and he got up to preach with a sailor's outfit on, with a Bible in one hand and a hymn book in the other. Someone yelled from the crowd, "Get down John, you are losing your mind." And John replied, " You are right, I probably am losing my mind, but there is one thing that I shall never forget; I was a great sinner, and Christ is a wonderful Savior." They let him finish his sermon.

Enjoy Jesus in Prayer

This work is a result of what God has done in my own personal life, and what is still is doing. I don't think I have to start quoting verses for you to realize how much prayer is mentioned in the Old and New Testaments. It was a way of life for the religious Jews to pray to the God of Israel. There are two very important Hebrew names for God that describe His care for His people. *Jehovah Shammah,* "The Lord is there, the Lord is My Companion." God's presence is not limited to a church building or a temple, but He is accessible to all who love and obey Him, because the blood of His Son has been shed on the cross. We can come boldly to the throne of grace (Heb. 10:19). Another powerful Hebrew name for God is *El Roi,* "The God Who Sees Me." There is not a circumstance in our life that escapes the all-knowing God. God knows us, and He knows when we are in trouble.

It is a great mystery how we can be on earth, and utter a prayer, and God hears us from Heaven, but it is true. That's why it is so crucial that we prayer with a sincere heart, because God is listening. Jesus condemned many of the Pharisees for pretending to pray (Mark 12:40). Sometimes I wonder how many of our public prayers reach to God. Prayer is such a intimate gift from God that Jesus said we should enter into our closet (Matt. 6:6). Every time I think of that verse, it reminds me of one of my great grandmothers, who raised my father. She never had any money, and the clothes she wore were many times gathered from the local garbage heap. She was not a beautiful woman to look upon, and she was somewhat crippled, with a disease of the spine. But she would go into the closet of her shack and pray all night for the needs of the family. I remember going to her house as a boy, and joy was always on her face. She read my father the Scriptures, and I believe to this very day that her prayers are being answered even today in my life.

Folks, prayer is not supposed to be just something we do with our heads bowed and our eyes closed. Prayer is having communication with the God of the universe, through faith in His Son, Jesus Christ. I have learned to go outside and lift up my eyes to the heavens, with my hands outstretched, and talk to God. That is the way Jesus did it (John 17:1). When we travel to Israel each year, I absolutely love the hills and mountains of Galilee, because the Bible says Jesus of Nazareth not only walked those hills, but He spent the night in those hills and prayed to His Father.

We need to designate a place and time to pray to God, and to be in a state of expectancy and joy when we pray. Believe without doubt, and be willing to accept God's will, because He knows best. There are those today who would have us to believe that you can just order God around, and send Him over here and over there. I try to be careful about telling God to give me this, or to give me that. I always say, "Lord, may your kingdom be advanced through my prayer." The Lord knows how selfish and greedy we are, but He also knows when we sincerely desire for Him to receive honor and glory. There are times in the Scriptures where God received glory in people being healed, and there were times when God received glory in people being sick (John 11:4; 2 Cor. 12:1–10). Even Jesus prayed, "Not my will by thine be done," in the Garden of Gethsemane. It was the Father's will for Jesus to die on the cross, but just think of the results. Salvation has come to the world through His death and resurrection.

Try to pray to God driving down the road, when you are taking a bath, before you go to sleep, when you get up in the morning. Before you go to church say a prayer for the minister and the people, and for God to touch you and your family. Pray before you witness to someone, that God will soften their hearts. Pray for those who are against you. Pray for those who talk bad about you, and remember those that walk in darkness cannot see where they are going. Pray before you exchange in a business adventure. Ask God what is best for not only yourself, but for the other person. Pray for God to bless your brothers and sisters in Christ.

But also remember that while we are commanded to pray for others, they still have to obey the Lord themselves. I recall one of my old preacher friends telling me about a lady who was lost, and every Sunday she would leave the church services asking him, "Pray for me pastor," "Pray for me pastor." After months and months, one Sunday she left and said again, "Pray for me pastor," and he replied, "I'm not going to pray for you anymore, it's time you stopped asking me that, and believe on the Lord Jesus Christ." She was saved the next week! So we need to put feet to our prayers as well.

One of my prayers for years has been for the Lord to bless me financially so I could bless His people. I still have very little compared to many people, but I still try to give to others as much as I can, in many different ways. It's hard for me to desire to be rich for myself when our Lord Jesus had nothing. But if He gives it to me, I hope I will be close enough to Him to give it away. But I find joy in talking to the Lord about it, and He knows what's best for me, and He knows how I would use it. I've met many people in hospital rooms who were sick, and they wanted me to pray for their healing, and I would. Sometimes they would be restored back to health, but then they would go back to their old sinful lifestyle all over again.

But learn how to enjoy talking to the Lord. Realize that Jesus died on the cross and rose again to give you the assurance that a "new and living way" has been made available to you. You do not have to pray through a priest; you become a priest when you accept Christ, and you have free access to the Father in Heaven (1 Pet. 2:9). Jesus made the supreme sacrifice for us on the cross, and our sacrifice to God now is a "sacrifice of praise" (Heb. 13:15–16).

Learn how to spend time with Jesus, He wants to hear from you. Do you recall the story of the two men on the road to Emmaus (Luke 24)? When Jesus walked with them, He saw their sad faces and He wanted them to tell Him the whole reason they were sad. They began to tell Jesus about this one who they had hoped was the Messiah, how He was crucified and was buried, and the women that were with them could not find His body. They did not realize that the one they were talking about was walking with them. Jesus wanted to hear it from their lips.

Jesus already knows what we need, folks, but He wants to hear it from us. One of the main reasons I believe is because God knows the joy that it will bring to our own life when we pray to Him. There is a joy released into our hearts when we spend time alone with God. Pray, pray, pray, and enjoy the work that Jesus has done to make it possible!

Enjoy Jesus in Music

Praise ye the Lord. Sing unto the Lord a new song, and his praise in the congregation of saints. Let Israel rejoice in him that made him: let the children of Zion be joyful in their King. Let them praise his name in the dance: let them sing praises unto him with the timbrel and harp.

—Psalm 149:1–3

Praise him with the sound of the trumpet: praise him with the psaltery and harp. Praise him with the timbrel and dance: praise him with stringed instruments and organs. Praise him upon the loud cymbals: praise him upon the high sounding cymbals. Let everything that hath breath praise the Lord. Praise ye the Lord.

—Psalm 150:3–6

After David had experienced the Lord's protection, and had received forgiveness, he is constantly praising the Lord. We would not have those beautiful praise psalms without God touching David's life. David was very gifted with the harp, and it is recorded in 1 Samuel 16:23, "And it came to pass, when the evil spirit from God was upon Saul, that David took an harp, and played with his hand: so Saul was refreshed, and was well, and the evil spirit departed from him." When David thought about how good the Lord had been to him, and how good God had been to Israel, he is bursting forth with jubilation. Is that not what we are supposed to do? When we think back on our lives, and see how gracious the Lord has been to us, how can we keep from praising God? When we read about Jesus giving His life on the cross for us, and how the resurrection assures us of life everlasting, how can we not praise the Lord? Singing and music can be a wonderful way to enjoy Jesus. Not focusing on the talent itself, but "singing unto the Lord" for all the great things He has done for us.

It is recorded in the gospels where after Jesus ate the last supper with his disciples in Jerusalem, "And when they had sung an hymn, they went out into the mount of Olives" (Matt. 26:30). They probably sang one of the psalms. Can you just imagine hearing the voice of Jesus? In the parable of the prodigal son, it is said that when the wayward son came home, they killed the fatted calf, and had a celebration with "music and dancing" (Luke 15:25). The apostle Paul was writing to the church in Colosse, and he told them, "Let the word of Christ dwell in you richly in all wisdom; teaching and admonishing one another in psalms and hymns and spiritual songs, singing with grace in your hearts to the Lord" (Col. 3:16).

While it is true that many churches have taken music

too far, and are trying to build a spiritual church on music itself, this does not take away the fact that music can be a powerful way to express our love to the Lord, and a way to minister to others. God created us with a heartstring that can be touched by music.

Music has been a part of my life as far back as I can remember. My father played several instruments, and he taught me how to play the guitar when I was a small boy. Little did I know that God was using the gift of music to minister to so many people through my singing. I am not an accomplished musician, but over the years the Lord has given me many songs to bless His people with. Thousands of testimonies over the years have been sent in to our office where people's lives were changed through the message of Christ in a song. While music should never be a substitute for the Scriptures, music crosses all barriers and denominational walls, and touches people of all ages. There are some people who will listen to a song quicker than they will a preached sermon. Whether it be watching television in their living room, or listening to radio driving down the road, music is a powerful tool that God has used to encourage His children.

I recall one testimony in particular, where a lawyer wrote me a letter from Illinois, and he and his wife had just been divorced. He couldn't deal with the loss, so he took a loaded gun in his car, and started down the road, and somewhere he was planning on ending his life. While on the highway, one of my songs came on the radio, and through the drawing of the Holy Spirit, he pulled the car off and surrendered his life to Christ. He told me to please keep singing the songs, because there were people like him who might never hear a preached sermon at church.

There is no room for prideful, egotistical musicians or singers in God's service, because all the glory must go to God. We must be very careful about trying to lift up ourselves, and make sure that Christ is exalted, and the words can be easily understood. Much of professional Christian music today is all about money and popularity. But many songs have been written over the years that were deeply inspired, and you can still feel that inspiration today. I have in my personal study some messianic Jewish music that seems to really help me to enjoy Jesus. So whatever style of music you prefer, find some music that exalts Christ and make it a part of your daily walk with God. Maybe taking a walk with a battery radio down a country road, or listening to music going to work, filling your heart with good thoughts before you go out into the world.

After Christ came into my heart, He took the desire away from me to listen to worldly music, and he replaced it with a desire to listen to music that brings me closer to Himself. There are times that I just have to lift my hands and shout, "Praise God" when I feel the Holy Spirit touching me. I feel sorry for so many people who do not know how to praise the Lord. God reveals deep truths to us many times when we are praising Him in music. I had a neighbor once who condemned me for playing my guitar in church, but he thought it was okay to play worldly music on my guitar. People who do not know the joy of music, most of the time are very sad people to be around. His comment was, "There is no mention of instruments in the New Testament." Well, there's no mention of a car either, but that does not make it sinful to drive one to church. There is no mention of a song book, but that does make it sinful to have one in the church. There is no mention of a baptistry, but most churches have them today. Some people "strain at a gnat, and swallow a camel," and miss the whole point. It's what we have in our heart that counts.

In the time of Jesus, music was a part of daily life, as well as temple worship. When the Jewish feasts were held, music was always a major part of the festivities. The people who think that it is wrong to have instruments in the church are going to be shocked if they get to Heaven.

And when he had taken the book, the four beasts and four and twenty elders fell down before the Lamb, having every one of them harps.

— Revelation 5:8

And I heard a voice from heaven, as the voice of many waters, and as the voice of a great thunder: and I heard the voice of harpers harping with their harps.

—Revelation 14:2

And I saw as it were a sea of glass mingled with fire: and

them that had gotten the victory over the beast, and over his image, and over his mark, and over the number of his name, stand on the sea of glass, having the harps of God. And they sing a song of Moses the servant of God, and the song of the Lamb, saying, Great and marvelous are thy works, Lord God Almighty, just and true are thy ways, thou King of saints.

—Revelation 15:2–3

Music will be in Heaven, because it pleases God when His creation praises Him. And all of the saints of God will praise Him throughout all of eternity. Don't you think it's time that we get started praising the Lord on earth?

Enjoying Jesus in Creation

We need to be reminded that sometimes we are guilty of worshiping the "Jesus" of our particular church, and not the Jesus of the Bible. When we do this, we are worshiping a very small Jesus. Some people think that Jesus is the perfect "Baptist," or the perfect "Methodist," or the perfect "Pentecostal," or the perfect "Church of Christ," or the perfect "Catholic," and our minds are blinded from the true, biblical Jesus. We all have been guilty of wanting Jesus to be what we wanted Him to be, instead of who He really is. But when we read the gospel of John, for example, we find that Jesus is none other than God Himself, the Creator of the universe.

John starts his gospel like this: "In the beginning was the Word, and the Word was with God, and the Word was God" (John 1:1). This takes us back to the very first verse in the Bible, "In the beginning, God created the heaven and the earth" (Gen. 1:1). John goes on to say, "All things were made by him; and without him was not any thing made that was made" (John 1:3). Have you ever thought of Jesus being the Creator of everything? "He was in the world, and the world was made by him, and the world knew him not" (John 1:10). It always moves me deeply to read that verse, just to think that Jesus came into a world that He created, and most of the world did not recognize who He was. There is an old gospel song that says, "He grew the tree, that he knew would be, used to make the old rugged cross." All of creation was made by our Lord Jesus.

It helps us to enjoy Jesus more when we realize that He is the Creator! Have you ever wondered what it meant when Jesus calmed the raging storm in Matthew 8:23–27? What about when He walked on the Sea of Galilee in John 6:15–21? This was telling the disciples, and telling you and me, that Jesus of Nazareth was none other than *Elohim,* "The All–powerful Creator." He had control over nature because He created it all. "Who hath measured the waters in the hollow of his hand, and meted out heaven with the span, and comprehended the dust of the earth in a measure, and weighed the mountains in scales, and the hills in a balance?" (Isa. 40:12). That was Jesus, my friend! And to just think of how He humbled Himself! He didn't walk on the water every time He went across the Sea of Galilee, but He could have. All of this is helping us to learn more about our Savior so we can enjoy Him to the fullest. When we see a beautiful sunrise, when we see a blue sky with white clouds, or feel the wind blow, or see the rain watering the earth, or a starry sky, and the moon shining its glistening rays across the earth, we can enjoy Jesus in creation.

Enjoying Jesus in creation helps us to see that not only

has He created everything for us to enjoy, but He has the power to keep this universe orchestrating daily, and that means that He can most assuredly take care of His children. Isn't that what Jesus was telling us in the Sermon on the Mount? We are to consider the flowers, and we are to look at the birds, and realize that since God takes care of them, how much more will He take care of His children?

We need to learn how to enjoy Jesus by seeing His handiwork all around us. As I am writing this book, I can see the wonderful autumn colors in the trees outside my window, and I think of how Jesus has colored my life with so many wonderful miracles. The same person who created everything has created a new person inside of me. He is in the creating business. This was the meaning of the miracle when Jesus turned the water into wine in John 2. No sunshine was needed, no grapes needed, no process of time needed; Jesus created wine out of water, showing forth His glory. This is why the Scriptures tell us, "Therefore if any man be in Christ, he is a **new creature;** old things are passed away; behold, all things are become new" (2 Cor. 5:17). Just like the Lord can take a dull, frostbitten tree with no leaves, and create a beautiful, green–leafed tree in the spring, He takes our dull life that has been scarred by sin and selfishness, with no purpose and no meaning, and creates something that He can use for His kingdom. He gives a fresh start in life, and not only that, He gives us a place of service and— like creation around us—we can glorify Him.

So let's not let our lives become so busy with the temporal things, and miss the eternal things. May we enjoy Jesus each and every day through His creation. May we start noticing His beauty all around us, and remember how powerful He is, and that He has allowed us to be born into this world, for one reason, to enjoy Him forever!

Enjoying Jesus in Art

Even though we should never worship pictures, statues, or any other man–made idea of what Jesus looked like, there is something to be said about Christian art, and it can help us to enjoy our Lord in a positive way.

Each era of history has tried to capture the precious Savior, and you can find many different ideas, such as pictures of Jesus from the Catholic traditions, to the Dark Ages, to the Reformation period, the Puritans, even up to the modern day. You can even find pictures of Jesus that depict Him as being a Chinese, African American, or maybe a blond–haired, blue–eyed, Hollywood movie star. But when we keep our Lord in His proper setting, He was a first–century Jew who grew up in Galilee. He would have been an olive–skinned Galilean, probably of normal stature, living among the common people of His day. Listen to what the prophet Isaiah said: "For he shall grow up before him as a tender plant, and as a root out of dry ground: he hath no form nor comeliness; and when we shall see him, there is no beauty that we should desire him" (Isa. 53:2).

This verse tells us that Jesus of Nazareth was a humble

looking man. He was not handsome, as some people would think, but His glory and His compassion drew people to Him from everywhere. Try to imagine living in the early first century in a remote part of the world, like Israel, where there were no televisions, no radio, no newspapers, no ways of modern communication. And yet, Jesus was a phenomenon! Multitudes of people were coming from all the regions in and around Galilee to see and to hear this man called *Yeshua!* So as we try to enjoy Jesus each day, if we can, surround ourselves with good, tasteful, images of the Jesus of the Scriptures.

In my personal study, I have a picture that was given to me by my sister–in–law, of Jesus sitting and overlooking Jerusalem. It stirs my heart, and makes me think of the passage where Jesus wept over Jerusalem. There is a picture to the left of my desk that was given to me by one of the churches where I preached a revival showing Jesus on the shores of Galilee teaching His disciples, and it reminds me of the close relationship that Jesus had with the twelve. They walked with Him; they talked with Him; they heard those beautiful parables; they saw the awesome miracles; and He taught them all about who He was and the kingdom of God. Those men turned the world upside down for Jesus the Messiah!

Sitting in the window, there is a picture of Jesus and the two men on the road to Emmaus, which is one of my favorite episodes in the life of Christ. I can't see that picture without thinking of Jesus walking with those two men, and as they started out, He hid Himself from them, but as they went along, He revealed to them that he was the long–awaited Messiah. Jesus took the *Tanakh*, the Old Testament, and expounded on all the things that were pertaining to His first coming. The greatest sermon that was ever given was given to two men on a dusty road. Then when they got to the village, Jesus made as though He would pass them on by, but in reality He just wanted them to invite Him into their home, and they did. When they broke bread together, there was something about the way Jesus prayed, or the way He broke the bread, or maybe they saw the scars in His hands—we do not know—but they recognized that Jesus was risen from the dead. Can't you say, "Glory to God"? Every time I read that story, it goes all through me, and that picture keeps me reminded of that story.

I did a concert for a Christian bookstore one time, and in return they sent me a beautiful water fountain that sits in my study of Jesus and the Samaritan woman. At the bottom of the fountain it reads: " If anyone is thirsty, let him come to me and drink" (John 7:37).

The conversation that Jesus had with the Samaritan woman is one of the richest in the Bible. How Jesus deliberately went through a part of Israel that was no–mans land in the time of Jesus. He knew the woman would be there at noonday, because she did not want to come at the normal time, in the late afternoon. She had a bad reputation: her life had been filled with multiple marriages, and she was living with a man. But our gracious and merciful

Lord took that woman from where she was, told her that He was the Messiah, and she forgot all about the physical water that she came to draw. She had tasted of the living water. She ran back to the town, and a great revival broke out as a result of her talking with Jesus. Jesus was showing His disciples that the kingdom was not only for the Jews, but for the Gentiles as well. What encouragement we find, knowing that Jesus does not condemn us for our failures in life. He came to save us. Can you say, "Glory to God"? That little fountain keeps me reminded of that powerful chapter in the gospels.

Over the window I have a old picture that most of you probably have seen, of Jesus holding a little sheep and hundred of other sheep are following behind. Need I say more? Just read the tenth chapter of John, and hear how Jesus talks about His sheep, and how He gives them eternal life, and how He has other sheep (Gentiles) who must be brought into the fold. Or what about the story in Luke 15 where He goes after that one lost sheep, and He searches until He finds it? Aren't you glad that Jesus came looking for you? Aren't you glad that He did not give up on you? What a blessing and what comfort it brings, to know that we are in the arms of precious Jesus! That picture keeps that thought in my mind and heart each day.

To the far wall of my study there hangs an eight–foot by eight–foot canvas painting of Jesus teaching from a boat on the Sea of Galilee. A multitude of people are on the shore, and two of His disciples are in the boat with Him.

Matthew 13 has long been one of my favorite passages to preach, where Jesus gave the mysteries of the kingdom of Heaven. This painting is so well done that every face speaks a thousand words, and even the birds flying over the water brings so many memories of our Holy Land trips. It took a wonderful Christian lady six months to paint it, but it has helped to stir praise and worship for Jesus that will last for eternity. I can't go into my study without thinking of Jesus on the shore of Galilee.

Not to mention many other pictures of Israel, Jewish menorahs, and Roman artifacts, that help me to enjoy the biblical Jesus.

Enjoying Jesus in Others

One of the strongest verses in the Old Testament is, "Thou shalt love thy neighbor as thyself" (Lev. 19:18). Jesus quoted that same verse in Mark 12:31, and the word for "love" in Hebrew is *ahab,* which is a very powerful word that means love in the deepest sense of the word. When you do word studies, most of the time they will give you the Greek word *agapao,* which is not the same. Just another perfect example that when studying the Scriptures, we should always search out the Hebrew words, because that was the original language of the Old Testament, and the primary language of Jesus. Sometimes the Greek word matches the Hebrew meaning, sometimes it does not.

The point I want to make is this: we are to love our neighbor as ourselves! Folks, that is strong indeed. The only way that is possible is for us to live a life filled with the Holy Spirit. If we live a life of carnality, we will be envious of our brothers and our sisters. The flesh is so sinful that most of us never learn how to control things like pride, ego, envy, selfishness, always drawing attention to ourselves. But when we start walking with Jesus we find a supernatural love for people. As we grow in Jesus, we grow to love people more and more, why? Because God lives in people! "For ye are the temple of the living God; as God hath said, I will dwell in them, and walk in them; and I will be their God, and they shall be my people" (2 Cor. 6:16).

There is no way that we can be filled with Jesus Christ and not love people. One way we can tell when we are really growing as believers, is when we can praise God for what He is doing in other people's lives. When we can enjoy seeing Jesus using other people as well as ourselves.

Can I be honest with you? When I went into the ministry, I was so naive I thought that all the preachers were going to love me and were going to help me, but I found more jealousy in the ministry than any other place. Satan is the author of jealousy, and he works overtime on ministers. We get caught up in our own little world, and we think we are God's gift to the world, and no one can do what we do. Let me tell you something, friends. God has children all over this world who are serving Him, and many of them are closer to Christ than we are. The American culture has programmed our thinking about big ministries, big churches, and "what's in this thing for me." But our hearts and minds are supposed to be on God's kingdom; it's not about me or you, it's all about enlarging God's kingdom! It's not about my ministry, or your church, it's about Christ and His eternal business!

One way we can promote God's kingdom is to invest some of our time and energy in what others are doing. Pray for God to raise up men and women, boys and girls, who will carry their cross for our Lord. Ask the Lord to bless His children, so that Jesus will be real in their lives. Give to promote other people's ministries, because they are just as important as ours, especially when they are sound in their doctrine, and we sense the power of God on their lives.

Can you thank God for blessing the brethren? Can you say, "Thank you, Lord," for giving my sister a bigger house than I've got? Can you thank the Lord for blessing your brother with a nicer car than you've got? And more important, can you praise the Lord for giving someone a greater understanding of God's Word than you've got? "We know that we have passed from death unto life, because we love the brethren. He that loveth not his brother abideth in death" (1 John 3:14).

When I see someone who seems to be close to God, I want to be around that person and ask God to teach me some things. Just because a person has been a Christian for many years does not mean that they know a lot about the Lord. Sometimes God will raise up a younger person who will teach older believers new truths. It's not how long we have been serving the Lord that counts, it's what we do with the time we have (Matt. 20:1–16).

Enjoy seeing Jesus in others. Enjoy seeing God bless His children. I want to see God's kingdom come, and I want to see Jesus pleased, and I want to see others serving our Lord. I'm thankful for what He has done for me, and what He has given me, but I have a great responsibility to use those gifts to help others as well. Our churches are filled with immature Christians who want credit and glory for everything they do. Their motive is all wrong, and their hearts are not in tune with the Lord. Let me tell you something: all the credit and glory belongs to the one who died on that cross for our sins. "But God forbid that I should glory, save in the cross of our Lord Jesus Christ" (Gal. 6:14).

Let's strive to be filled with God's Holy Spirit so that He can love others through us. May we all learn how to enjoy Jesus working in the lives of His children, because this is pleasing to God, and I want to please Him!

Enjoying Jesus in Preaching

And I, if I be lifted up from the earth, will draw all men
unto me.

—John 12:32

Even though it may sound strange to us, Jesus dying on
a cross would be the thing that would draw people to salvation. That is why it is crucial that we preach Christ and
Him crucified (1 Cor. 2:2). It's getting harder and harder to
hear a good sermon about Jesus, His earthly ministry, and
His death, burial, and resurrection. The modern world has
turned biblical Christianity into things like: how to grow a
church, or how to be healthy, or how to be wealthy, or we
get caught up in water baptism, election, or what the Bible
might say about this or that. We are to preach on the Savior,
my friends! When preaching is exalting Christ, then it is
enjoyable.

One reason I think so many people do not enjoy coming to church anymore is because they are tired of hearing
the social gospel of our day. People are hungering for the
person of Jesus the Messiah. When preaching is filled with

Jesus and the power of the Holy Spirit, it is the most wonderful thing in the world. What a blessing it is to hear a sermon about the prophecies concerning the coming Messiah, and then show me where they are fulfilled in the New Testament. To hear a sermon on the virgin birth of Christ thrills my soul, to see how God orchestrated the events in history to bring His Son into the world. How I enjoy hearing about the earthly ministry of Jesus, how He raised the dead, healed the sick, caused blinded eyes to see, calmed a raging storm, and walked on the water. My heart leaps inside of me when I hear a sermon about Jesus sitting in a boat and preaching about the kingdom of God on the shore of Galilee. For someone to explain the parables that Jesus gave sets my soul on fire. And for a preacher to tell me that God loved me so much that He gave His only begotten Son to die on a cross for my sins, brings joy to my life and tears to my eyes. When I hear that Jesus not only died, but He rose again, gives me the assurance that I've got everlasting life, wow!

If there ever was a time when people need to hear sermons about sweet Jesus, it is now. We don't need preachers who just choose to go into the ministry as a vocation; we need God–called preachers. We don't need preachers to give us denominational jargon; we need preachers to give us Christ.

. . . And how shall they hear without a preacher? And how shall they preach, except they be sent? as it is written,

How beautiful are the feet of them that preach the gospel of peace, and bring glad tidings of good things!

—Romans 10:14b–15

This little book is about how to enjoy Jesus, and I can tell you from experience that sitting under the sound of good preaching is crucial. Why? "So then faith cometh by hearing, and hearing by the word of God" (Rom. 10:17). Jesus-filled preaching not only gives lost people faith to trust in Christ for salvation, but it increases the believer's faith so we can grow in grace and knowledge of our Lord. Find yourself a good Bible–believing, gospel–preaching church, and if you can't find one, listen to sermons at home, and feed that inner man with the meat of God's Word. Learn to enjoy hearing messages about Jesus the Messiah!

Enjoying Living a Godly Life

So many professing believers struggle with trying to live a godly life. Many have approached me over the years and said, "Brother Carroll, I just can't live this Christian life; it's too hard for me." Well, not trying to sound judgmental, but I'm afraid their motive was all wrong. Living a godly life is not in struggling in the flesh to be good and trying to stay away from sin, or just in being a moral person. It is in walking so close to our Lord Jesus Christ that the Holy Spirit lives that life through us, and sometimes we are not even aware of it.

Many times we are like the Jews of old, and we get to thinking that we must be living a godly life if we are prospering in this world. "Supposing that gain is godliness" (1 Tim. 6:5). Many people think that financial prosperity is the sign of God's blessing, but according to the Scriptures, that is not always the case. This is what the Pharisees thought in the time of Jesus; the Messiah was born in poverty, lived in poverty, and died on a cross. We must guard ourselves from this kind of thinking. Why? Because if we fall into this way of thinking, then when hard times hit, or our finances are depleted, then we go into a state of depression, and we feel as though we have done something wrong and God is punishing us, and this has happened to countless people.

The Scriptures tell us that in the last days that people will "have a form of godliness, but denying the power thereof" (2 Tim. 3:5). This is when people are worried about looking godly, appearing to be godly, but inside they are not truly born–again. Our churches are filled with people like this who only have a form of godliness, but they do not have the power of the Holy Spirit.

> For the grace of God that bringeth salvation hath appeared to all men, teaching us that, denying ungodliness and worldly lusts, we should live soberly, righteously, and godly, in this present evil world. Looking for that blessed hope, and the glorious appearing of the great God and our Savior Jesus Christ. Who gave himself for us, that he might redeem us from all iniquity, and purify unto himself a peculiar people, zealous of good works.
>
> —Titus 2:11–14

So here we have the biblical answer to living a godly life. It is the **grace of God** that brought salvation to mankind; it was not something we did for ourselves, or something that we deserve. It was His everlasting love for us, not our love for Him. It was His mercy, His kindness, His coming down to us that saved us. Once we have received that wonderful, mysterious **grace of God,** through Christ our Lord, then we will have the power to deny ungodliness and worldly lusts. We can live **in** this sinful, fallen world, and not be **of** this world. One of the best ways to live godly is to **look** for the second coming of the Messiah each day of our lives. God's glory was manifested in the Old Testament as a "pillar of fire," as a "cloud," as God followed the children of Israel. God's glory was manifested in the tabernacle, in the temple that Solomon built, but the prophet Ezekiel saw the glory of God depart from the temple, and go to the east, on the Mount Of Olives. Well, dear brethren, Jesus of Nazareth was the manifestation of God's glory, and when He left this earth in a cloud, He was on the Mount of Olives. That same Jesus is going to return, and His glory will come back to Jerusalem, and the whole earth will be filled with His glory! I don't think many believers are aware of what glory awaits us when we see Jesus face to face. We have a **blessed hope** that Christ will appear in our lifetime, and if not in our lifetime, we will go to meet Him. It's going to be a **glorious** appearance when He comes, and if we are living close enough to Him that we can pray, "Even so, come Lord Jesus," then our lives will be filled with godliness.

If we live a godly life in this world, we will be a **peculiar** people, but that is the key. We are not supposed to be like everybody else. Rejoice in being what God has called you to be. Christ has shed His blood on the cross, and he has redeemed us from our sins, and has purified us unto Himself. I belong to Jesus, praise God! Why would I not want to live for Him? Why would I not want to make my life count for Him?

Living for Jesus Christ is something to enjoy, folks. Enjoy being set free from your sins, and not being what you used to be. Enjoy not going to those same places anymore, enjoy not talking the way you used to talk. Thank God for your new life in Christ! Enjoy seeing where God has brought you, and enjoy where he will take you in the future. Enjoy the ride! Jesus told His disciples when they were in a boat on the Sea of Galilee, "Let us pass over unto the other side" (Mark 4:35). They went through a storm, but they did get to the other side. When Jesus tells us that we will be with Him one day, we will be with Him; He cannot lie. So enjoy living each day to the fullest for Christ. May we all strive to be as godly as we can, through God's power and grace. And you know what I have discovered? I have a long way to go to be what I need to be, but I never thought that I would be as far along as I am. We can be more like Christ than we think we can. Don't settle for nominal Christianity; see how far He will take you. Enjoy living for Jesus!

Enjoy Jesus Being Your Provider

One of the things that prevent many people from enjoying Jesus is worry. Jesus plainly told us in Matthew 6:25–34 not to be anxious about the cares of life. And He chose from the animal life a bird, and from the plant life a flower to illustrate His point. Birds only weigh a few ounces, and yet they eat pounds and pounds of food. Why is this? Because the physiology and metabolism of a bird is totally different than us humans. They eat constantly, and God provides for them. How much more, Jesus said, will He take care of us. A flower in the field is not even planted by a man, it grows wild, and yet, it has more beauty than even King Solomon had in his day. If God would clothe a flower that grows wild in the field, how much more will He clothe us, His children.

One of the best scriptures to show how God provides for His children is also the Twenty–third Psalm. Many times old, familiar passages of Scripture are where God speaks to us the loudest because we think we've already learned that passage, and in reality, we never really got what He was saying to us. I would like to take this familiar psalm and I pray

How to Enjoy Jesus

that God will do a knew thing in your life, and take away your worries and fears.

> The Lord is my shepherd; I shall not want. He maketh me to lie down in green pastures: he leadeth me beside the still waters. He restoreth my soul: he leadeth me in the paths of righteousness for his name's sake. Yea, though I walk through the valley of the shadow of death, I will fear no evil: for thou art with me; thy rod and thy staff they comfort me. Thou preparest a table before me in the presence of mine enemies: thou anointest my head with oil; my cup runneth over. Surely goodness and mercy shall follow me all the days of my life: and I will dwell in the house of the Lord forever.

Psalms in Hebrew is *tehillim* (praise) or *tehillot* (prayer). So these psalms are praises or prayers unto the Lord. David had lived a life of a shepherd, and David knew everything about being a shepherd. That little shepherd boy not only killed the giant Goliath, he became one of the greatest kings in the history of Israel. The people saw little David as just a shepherd boy, but God saw him as a king! And the Messiah, *Yeshua*, is called the Son of David. David had no idea that God was preparing him so he could write this psalm that would comfort and bless millions of people down through the centuries of time.

The Lord is my shepherd—*Yehovah Rohi!* When we need forgiveness of our sins and we need God's righteousness, His name is *Yehovah Tsidkenu*. When we need healing, His name is *Yehovah Rapha*. But when we need a provider to lead and to care for us, His name is *Yehovah Rohi*.

The pagan gods were so unapproachable, and so impersonal. But the God of David, and the God of Israel, wants to be our personal Shepherd! Sheep in the land of Israel have to have a shepherd, they are lost without a shepherd, and if we try to go through this life without trusting God to be our shepherd, we too are in big trouble, and we will worry our entire life trying to take care of ourselves.

I shall not want—What does that mean? It means that we will not want for anything! The Lord is my provider, and he knows what I need even before I ask Him. You see, sheep cannot protect themselves, they cannot provide for themselves, and David is using this metaphor to show us that God is his provider, and he lacks nothing. For us to try and live our life without God is like a sheep without a shepherd. We were created to depend on God, and if we unplug ourselves, we are dead. What is wrong with most of us, we are too independent, we need to be dependent on God. We are the sheep of His pasture. There is a God–shaped void in everyone's life until they come to know God through faith in Jesus Christ, and that void cannot be filled with money, business, pleasures, sex, alcohol, drugs, or anything else. Only God will satisfy that void in our lives. "As the hart panteth after the water brooks, so panteth my soul after thee, O God" (Ps. 42:1).

He maketh me to lie down in green pastures—

David is talking about the everyday needs of the sheep. Sheep have to have grass. In Israel, the rain comes from the west, off of the Mediterranean Sea, so the eastern slopes sometimes do not have any grass. The shepherd's job is to find those patches of grass on the slopes of the mountains. Just like a shepherd who finds grass for His sheep, God is concerned about those mundane, everyday needs of His people. He makes the sheep to lie down—this is a picture of contentment, the sheep do not lie down unless they are contented. If they are afraid, they will not lie down. If they are in a fight with other sheep, they will not lie down. If they are bothered with insects, or pests, they will not lie down. If they are hungry, they will not lie down. The shepherd gives them peace of mind. God gives His children peace of mind so we too can lie down in green pastures, and not worry about the everyday needs that we have.

He leadeth me beside the still waters—Sheep cannot drink in swift running water, so the shepherd finds the quite, still waters. They are beside still waters where the water is always close by. If the sheep are not close beside water, they will drift off and wild animals will get them, or they will fall off one of the sharp cliffs to their death.

He restoreth my soul—The sheep are restored physically when they get hungry. When they get tired, the shepherd gives them a renewed sense that they are being provided for. Think how God restores His children, even in the everyday things like eating a meal, having a cool drink when it is hot, or just being able to sit down after working hard all day. Also, think how God restores His children after we have sinned against Him and He provides forgiveness for us. What about when others do things against us? What about when we get discouraged about trouble in the church, or trouble in our families. God comes to restore us back to fellowship with Him. There is no need for a child of God to be depressed or downtrodden all of the time. "Why art thou cast down, O my soul"? (Ps. 42:5).

He leadeth me in the paths of righteousness for His name's sake—When we take our Israel tours each year, we see little pathways that have been trampled on all across the Judean mountains. That is where the shepherds have led their sheep across the paths to provide pasture, water, and protection. The shepherd has to be very careful and not let the sheep overgraze in one spot. Maybe the rain will come and wash away some of the top soil, or parasites from the sheep droppings will poison the sheep, or maybe wild animals have located the sheep. The shepherd has to keep the sheep moving. God does not want His children to stand still, my friend; He wants us to grow and to move forward. So many believers are just existing, they are not growing in the Scriptures, and they just become complacent. They lose their joy, and become worried again about their physical needs more so than their spiritual needs. Many times church people become comfortable, and they think they are doing fine, but in reality they are hiding behind the church and are not growing in grace and knowledge of the Lord Jesus Christ. What have you learned today about Christ?

Are you farther along in your Christian walk than you were a year ago?

God leads us in paths in righteousness "for his name's sake." The shepherd's name is on the line. If anything happens to the sheep, it all goes back to the shepherd's reputation. If we are following the Lord, it is His responsibility to provide for us. His name is on the line, and His name is holy, and He has not lost one sheep yet. God has a perfect track record. Always remember that God saves us, through Jesus, not because we are worthy, or because we deserve it, but it is for His name's sake!

Yea, though I walk through the valley of the shadow of death, I will fear no evil—The shepherd leads the sheep through many valleys, because water is there, and they can find a cool spot from the sun, but David picks out the darkest valley of all, the valley of the shadow of death. Why did he say it was only a "shadow"? Because it is an illusion! Death is not what it seems to be. Death seems to be a tragedy, but in reality, it is a triumph. The shepherd will not lead his sheep through a valley that he has not already walked through. Wow! Jesus the Messiah has already walked through the valley of death, and He came out victorious. He has already been there, and there is nothing to be afraid of. When physical death comes to the Lord's sheep, we just go on to live with Jesus. Not only did Jesus become a common man who lived and grew up in poverty, but He died our death and He walked out of the grave. Glory to God! Now, David did not say that he could walk around the valley of the shadow of death, he must go through it. God has not told us in the Scriptures that we would avoid the valleys; no, we must go through the valleys. There is sorrow to face, there is death to face, but Christ has already been there, and He will go with us through even death itself.

Thy rod and thy staff, they comfort me—There are two instruments of protection for the sheep that the shepherd uses—a rod and a staff. The rod is a short piece of a tree limb, or sometimes a three– or four–foot stick. This is used as a club to beat off the bears and the wolves from the sheep. Sometimes the shepherd tries to take a nap in the afternoon, and the wild animals will slip up and try to snatch one of the sheep. But listen to what the Bible says about our Lord: "Behold, he that keepeth Israel, shall neither slumber or sleep" (Ps. 121:4).

Also, the rod is used to count the sheep, as they come into the fold each night. It is called, "rodding the sheep." And if one sheep is lost, he closes the door of the sheepfold up, and he goes searching for that lost sheep until he finds it (Luke 15:3–7).

The rod is a symbol of authority, and that is why the Scriptures tell us that Jesus, the Son of God, will rule with "a rod of iron" in the book of the Revelation.

The staff is a long piece of wood, with a crook in the top. This is used to guide and to comfort the sheep. The crook fits the contour of the sheep's back, and he uses the staff to pull the sheep near to himself. Maybe the shepherd will lift the sheep out of a briar thicket with the staff. We need to draw near unto God, when we are in trouble, or when we need healing. His staff is a symbol of comfort and guidance. Many times over the years, I have had to draw near to God, and He has taken care of me many times, even when I couldn't take care of myself.

Thou preparest a table before me in the presence of mine enemies—Two meanings can be drawn from this. One, the shepherd goes in front of the sheep, and prepares the place where they are going to be eating. There are wild flowers in Israel that are beautiful on the outside, but they are poisonous. The shepherd has to clear off the poisonous flowers and weeds for the sheep so that they will not eat them and die, and the enemies will come to devour them. Also, in a social way, David had received the Lord's forgiveness, and God had taught him how to eat in the presence of his enemies. Eating with others in biblical times was a sign of acceptance, or forgiveness. This is why Jesus was always eating with people, He was showing them that He loved them, and He came to save them, not destroy them. You may recall how Jesus prepared breakfast for His disciples on the shore of Galilee even after they had scattered and after Peter had denied Him back in Jerusalem. He was telling them that He had forgiven them, and He restored them back to fellowship with Himself (John 21).

We overcome our enemies by loving them, not by rejecting them. We are to show the lost world what Christ has done for us, and sometimes it means even eating in the presence of our enemies.

Thou anointest my head with oil—This too, has two meanings that we can glean from. The shepherds would place olive oil on the faces of the little sheep in order to keep the flies from going up their noses and eating their brains out. Every good shepherd keeps a supply of olive oil on hand. Also, one of the ways to greet a special person in Bible times was by anointing their head with oil. Do you recall in 1 Samuel 16:13 how the prophet Samuel anointed the head of the little shepherd boy David? God told him to because that little shepherd boy would one day be the king of Israel. Do you recall Matthew 26, when the woman anointed the head of Jesus? She knew that He was the Messiah, a very special person to her, while Simon did not think Jesus was so special.

God is telling us that we are very special to Him, and when we come to know Him through our faith in Jesus the Messiah, He anoints us with the Holy Spirit, so the devil can't get us. Wow!

My cup runneth over—If you were living in Israel in those days and someone came to see you, you would examine that person as they ate with you. You were required to give them at least a small piece of bread, even if it was barley bread, the poorest means of bread. If you had any wine, you would give to them according to what you thought of that person. If they seemed dishonest or crafty, and you didn't really care for them, you would fill their cup only half-full of wine. But if you liked that person, you will fill the cup to overflow, and that would let that person know that they could stay overnight.

God is telling David, and telling His children, that He loves us, and we can live with Him forever. God sees something in us that He loves, even though we have failed Him, because Jesus, His Son, has paid the price for our sins, we have been accepted. My cup runneth over!

Surely goodness and mercy shall follow me all the days of my life; and I will dwell in the house of the Lord for ever—The word "follow" in Hebrew is *radaph*, and it means "to pursue, or chase down." God's goodness and mercy had been chasing David all the days of his life. When you read the story of David, from the time he was anointed by Samuel as a little boy, God protected David, and He watched over him, even when David sinned greatly. It is recorded that David was "a man after God's own heart" (1 Sam. 13:14). Not only did God's mercy and goodness pursue David in this life, but he would be with the Lord, forever!

The Lord in Heaven is not only our Provider in this life, But He has provided eternal salvation for all of His children. Would you like to make God your shepherd? Just repent of your sins and trust in Jesus of Nazareth as your personal Savior, and He will take care of you all the days of your life, and one day, you will be with Him!

Enjoy Jesus in Giving

> But this I say, He which soweth sparingly shall reap also
> sparingly; and he which soweth bountifully shall reap
> also bountifully. Every man according as he purposeth in
> his heart, so let him give; not grudgingly, or of necessity:
> for God loveth a cheerful giver.
>
> —2 Corinthians 9:6–7

While I do not believe that we are bound by the Jewish law
of tithing, we are told in the New Testament that we are to
be generous and to have a cheerful attitude about giving.
There seems to be a law of reciprocity in the Scriptures that
says if we give, God will give back to us. Now, that should
not be our motive, and many ministries today are exalting
prosperity, and they take Scriptures out of context in order
to get people to send money to their ministry. Neverthe-
less, God says if we give sparingly, we will reap sparingly, if
we give bountifully, we shall also reap bountifully. And we
are not to give with a sour look on our face, or give grudg-
ingly, but give cheerfully. So how do we give? To whom and
to what do we give?

Because the local church is a vital arm of God's kingdom, we need to support our local church so that the gospel
of Christ can carry on in our communities. We do need to
make sure that the church we attend teaches sound doctrine, and that the church is using God's money effective-
ly. I know this is not popular for me to say this, but the
western culture focuses on spending big money on buildings, fellowship halls, gymnasiums, etc., but I do not give
to these kinds of projects; I want to give where I know the
money will promote God's true kingdom, not a monument
for someone else. I also do not believe that all of our giving should go to the local church. When we give to God's
children we are giving unto the Lord as well. So many give
money to their church and they wouldn't walk across the
driveway and give money to a needy neighbor. I try to look
for opportunities to give to orphans, widows, the poor, and
I try to give generously. How many of you know that you
cannot out–give God? He has been so good to me that I
have to give to others.

> Bring ye all the tithes into the storehouse, that there
> may be meat in mine house, and prove me now herewith,
> saith the Lord of hosts, if I will not open you the win-
> dows of heaven, and pour you out a blessing, that there
> shall not be room enough to receive it.
>
> —Malachi 3:10

This verse has been used over the years to try and say that

all the tithes should come into the church. But the "store-house" was a place in the temple compound where they kept enough grain and meat to take care of the needy. Four hundred years before Jesus came, the Jewish people still lived under the law of Moses, and tithing was what was required by God, and He promised to bless them for their obedience.

The principle however, still remains that God will bless His children for being generous givers. "Give, and it shall be given unto you; good measure, pressed down, and shaken together, and running over, shall men give into your bo-som. For with the same measure that ye mete withal it shall be measured to you again" (Luke 6:38). In biblical times, they would store their grain in large containers, and they would pressed the grain down into the containers, shake it, press some more, and fill it to overflowing. This is the picture of what God will give to us, if we give!

Let me give you a personal testimony about giving. When I started traveling in the ministry, I had no place to go, no money, and a car that was worth about one hundred dollars. I knew the Lord had placed His call upon me to preach the gospel. I did not worry about money, I just prayed to the Lord that He would use me, and bless me, so I could bless others. I always tried to help those I saw in need on the road, even though I had little myself. But God would bring people into my life to help me, and He kept His work going through the giving of His children ("men shall give into your bosom"). I never had a desire to be wealthy, and I still don't, but God has blessed me more than I could ever explain. He has given me understanding of His Word, the power of His Spirit, given me gifts to use for His glory, love in my heart for the brethren, more places to go and minister than I could ever fulfill. He has taken our little ministry and now we are in over one hundred countries by means of Christian television, He has allowed me to take hundreds of people to Israel over the years, and even though I am not a rich man financially, I do have more finances than I ever thought I would have. If we are faithful in the little things, God will give us the big things. How could I not be a cheerful giver, after what God has done for me?

We are to enjoy Jesus in giving, and enjoy spreading the love of God around. Hey, folks, if I was a wealthy person, I would be blessing many people. I would be sending people to Israel, I would be giving to orphanages, and I would be looking for ways to make a difference in this ole world. But I will have to give an account of what I have done, and I have learned to enjoy Jesus in giving to others. I enjoy having that love in my heart for others. I enjoy seeing others be blessed, and I enjoy knowing that maybe I have done what the Lord wanted me to do. When the Lord puts it on my heart, I do not want anyone to rob me of a blessing.

Think of the contrast between the widow who gave two mites in Luke 21, and the rich young ruler in Luke 18 who would not give up his money in order to follow Christ. It wasn't how much she gave, or how much the ruler had, but it was their attitude toward giving. The widow loved the

Lord so much that she gave all she had. The rich young ruler thought he could live good enough morally to get to Heaven, and still keep his money. But Jesus was showing that when we are sincere followers, the attitude toward money will change. Almost three hundred verses are in the gospels concerning money, and we need to take a serious listen to what Christ is saying. For example, listen to Luke 16:9–11:

And I say unto you, Make to yourselves friends of the mammon of unrighteousness; that, when ye fail, they may receive you into everlasting habitations. He that is faithful in that which is least is faithful also in much; and he that is unjust in the least is unjust also in much. If therefore ye have not been faithful in the unrighteous mammon, who will commit to your trust the true riches?

If sin had not come into the world, we would not need money in the first place, so money is not the true riches. We are to take money and make friends with it that we will meet in Heaven one day. And if we do not use a temporary thing like money for good, then God will not give us eternal riches.

Enjoy Jesus in the Home

And the Lord said unto Noah, Come thou and all thy
house into the ark; for thee have I seen righteous before
me in this generation.

—Genesis 7:1

Any serious Bible student knows that the ark was a type
of Messiah, and as the days of Noah were rebellious and
wicked, so it will be when the Messiah returns the second
time. "As it was in the days of Noe, so shall it be also in the
days of the Son of man" (Luke 17:26). Noah was a preacher
of righteousness, and for one hundred and twenty years he
preached about the coming flood. But the people mocked
and laughed, as Noah kept on preaching and preparing the
ark. No one listened to Noah, but his family did. "In the self-
same day entered Noah, and Shem, and Ham, and Japheth,
the sons of Noah, and Noah's wife, and the three wives of
his sons with them, into the ark" (Gen. 7:13). This is a good
example that if we walk with God, that most people in the
world may ridicule us, and we will be a peculiar people to
the outside world. But we do have the responsibility, given

to us by God, to show our families the way to Heaven. They may not always follow, but show our families by example how to live for God.

What a wonderful, blessed thought, to think that my wife and children will be with me in Heaven one day. And we as the husbands and fathers must take the lead and live our faith before our families.

Wives, submit yourselves unto your own husbands, as unto the Lord. For the husband is the head of the wife, even as Christ is the head of the church: and he is the savior of the body. Therefore as the church is subject unto Christ, so let the wives be unto their own husbands in every thing. Husbands, love your wives, even as Christ also loved the church, and gave himself for it.

—Ephesians 5:22–25

God is telling us that Spirit–filled believers being married to each other, He compares to Christ and His church. That is a powerful comparison!

One of the major problems that we have in our religious society is that people substitute attending church for living the Christian life. The real test in when we get home, and how we live before our wives and children. I think the church as a whole has done a poor job addressing this problem. We are too interested in big ministries and looking good on the outside, instead of ministering to our own families. As I look back on my life, I wish had taken more time with my children as I was traveling so much in the ministry, but God has been merciful, and they are saved, and hopefully they will see Christ in me more in the future. We can enjoy Jesus in our homes, and we need to start today.

Learn how to talk with your wife and your husband about the things of Christ. Ask Bible questions to each other, and discuss what you really believe about eternal things. Learn how to bless your children instead of always correcting them. As they did in the days of Jesus, place your hands on your children, and say a blessing on their life. Ask God to protect them, to keep them from Satan, to lift up His face and shine upon them, and to bless their lives for His kingdom. Let them see your love for others, your generosity, your concern for God's business, and even if they don't follow immediately, they will never forget it, and one day they will come around. They may depart for a while, but we must plant some deep seeds of faith in their life while they are young.

When you say the blessing at meal time, be sure to humble yourself, and exalt Christ in your prayer, and seize the opportunity to be a blessing. No one wants to be around a know-it-all who always talks religion, but we can represent Christ in a nice way that tells our children that serving Jesus is wonderful, not a drudgery, or a boring, cover-up lifestyle. Many have shared with me over the years how their parents forced them to go to church, or forced them to read the Bible, and it made them bitter and resentful. Serving Jesus is supposed to be a joy, not a burden.

We must strive to make our homes a place of love, a place of peace, a place that the children will enjoy. We want to leave behind a legacy that proves that we loved Jesus Christ. Certainly there are times when we have problems, sometimes the wife or husband does not want to live for the Lord, or we may have a child that is wayward, but we still have a job to do, and we must do it.

One preacher was going through a village years ago, and he saw a man working in a field. He asked him, "Sir, are you a follower in Jesus," to which the man replied, " Why don't you go and ask my family." May our family see Jesus in us!

Enjoy Jesus in Eating

And the Pharisees and scribes murmured, saying, This
man receiveth sinners, and eateth with them.

—Luke 15:2

Then Jesus said unto them, Verily, verily, I say unto you,
Except ye eat the flesh of the Son of man, and drink his
blood, ye have no life in you.

—John 6:53

I am the bread of life.

—John 6:48

The religious people were complaining because Jesus was
eating with the tax collectors and the outcasts of the day.
Eating with them proved that Jesus did not come to condemn them, but He came to save them. The religious people
should have been rejoicing, but as always, religion blinded
them from the mission of the Messiah.

Jesus used the metaphor of eating and drinking to show
how we must receive Him into our lives. He was not talking

about cannibalism, but He was symbolizing that when we are truly born–again, He comes to live within our innermost being, like eating His flesh, and drinking His blood. God has given us the wonderful gift of being able to enjoy food, and digest the food. With that thought in mind, we can enjoy feasting on Jesus our Lord. "O taste and see that the Lord is good"! (Ps. 34:8).

It's very interesting to do word studies in the Hebrew language. And when you study the place where Jesus the Messiah was to be born, we find the place as *Beth–lehem Ephratah* (Mic. 5:2). Bethlehem means "house of bread," and then Jesus the Messiah proclaimed, *Anee Hoo Lechem Ha Chayim,* **"I am the bread of life"**! Jesus used the God–given gift of eating to illustrate how important He is to our life. Jesus is what life is all about. We cannot exist physically if we do not eat, and we cannot exist spiritually if we do not partake of Jesus, the Son of God! He is the reason we are here; He is what life is all about, and we are supposed to enjoy Him!

This subject may sound strange to us western–world Gentiles, but in Bible times eating was considered a very special time in the land of Israel. Life was very difficult, and if God did not send the rain on their crops, they were in big trouble. One of the signs of God's blessings was a good harvest, and a sign of God's punishment was famine.

And it shall come to pass, if ye shall hearken diligently unto my commandments which I command you this day, to love the Lord your God, and to serve him with all your heart and with all your soul, That I will give you the rain of your land in his due season, the first rain and the latter rain, that thou mayest gather in thy corn, and thy wine, and thine oil. And I will send grass in thy fields for thy cattle, that thou mayest eat and be full. Take heed to yourselves, that your heart be not deceived, and ye turn aside, and serve other gods, and worship them; And then the Lords' wrath be kindled against you, and he shut up the heaven, and that there be no rain, and that the land yield not her fruit; and lest ye perish quickly from off the good land which the Lord giveth you.

—Deuteronomy 11:13–17

This was the covenant that God made with Israel over fourteen hundred years before the coming of the Messiah into the world. So when the harvest was good, and the rains came, eating together was a special moment, and they enjoyed the blessings of the Lord.

Once we had a chance to eat a biblical meal in Nazareth, and they served us lentil soup, olives, and pita bread baked before us on an open fire. We know that Jesus ate fish and honeycomb after he was resurrected (Luke 24:42). Wine was the common drink because of the bacteria in the water. They would dilute the fermented wine with two-thirds water. The fruit in Israel is some of the sweetest in the world—oranges, dates, bananas, grapes, pomegranates, and melons, not to mention all variety of nuts. We all would be much healthier if we ate biblically. Even though we are not bound by that Mosaic law, there is a reason why God gave those dietary laws to Israel. We abuse our temples in the western culture with the way we eat, and it is a sin when people just turn into gluttons, and destroy the temple that God gave them. Many people have asked me to pray for their healing over the years after they had abused their bodies for years by overeating. If we sow to the flesh, we will reap the flesh.

But the point I want to make about eating is, we are supposed to enjoy Jesus when we eat. Realizing that the Lord has created the earth in a way that it will bring forth bread, fruits, and vegetables for us humans to eat. We know the prayer that Jesus prayed before he ate: *Baruch Atah Adonai Eliheinu Melech Ha Olam Ha Motzi Lechem Min Ha Eretz!* **Blessed Are You, O Lord Our God, King of the Universe, Who Bringeth Forth Bread From the Earth!** The emphasis is on thanking God for giving us the food from the earth that He has created, not just blessing the food itself. This is a powerful way to teach our families how to enjoy mealtime from a biblical perspective.

Eating in the time of Jesus was also a special time to have fellowship with each other. Enjoy learning more about each other, give encouragement to each other, and cherish the time God has given us to be together. It's not supposed to be just a quick, casual time when we just sit down and rush through it; enjoy eating, and enjoy eating with God's people.

Eating is something we must do every day, and enjoying Jesus is something we must do every day. It's those little things in life that become big things when we get our hearts right with God. No wonder the two men on the road to Emmaus said, "And they told what things were done in the way, and how he was known of them inbreaking of bread" (Luke 24:35).

Enjoy Jesus in the Church

We need to learn how to enjoy Jesus in our everyday private lives, and we also need to learn how to enjoy Jesus in our corporate lives as well. God wants us to fellowship with other believers. Some of the first century believers in *Yeshua* as Messiah were seriously thinking about withdrawing themselves from worshiping with the messianic believers and going back into Judaism. But the writer told them, "Not forsaking the assembling of ourselves together, as the manner of some is" (Heb. 10:25). But I think we can also see from that verse that the Lord does want us to gather together. I think it is important for us to determine what the "church" really is.

The church is the *kahal*, or, "the called–out ones." It is the body of born–again believers! It is the people who believe that Jesus of Nazareth is the Messiah, Jew or Gentile. It is not the building on the corner, or the denomination— the church is the people! The church belongs to Christ, not a preacher, or a board of deacons, or to someone who donated the most to the family life center. We gather together to worship Christ, and to encourage other believers. Church is a place where we exalt the crucified Redeemer, and He draws people to Himself.

It's so sad to see how the modern idea of church has drifted far from what Jesus intended it to be. Today, it's all about how nice the building is, or how many people are coming, or how big the budget is, or how much we pay the preacher, and we hang a sign out front that tells the people what kind of church we are. It's easy to see why so many are confused and discouraged with the church. There is only one true church, the church that Jesus the Messiah died for. Some groups think they have a monopoly on God, but they are going to be greatly disappointed one day to find out that God has children all over this world, from all different backgrounds. I have met some godly people in my travels over the years who do not believe exactly the way I do, who do not believe in the style of worship I do, who do not like the kind of music I like, and who believe in totally different ways of worship, but they were close to Christ, and they serve him faithfully. In America, we have all these different interpretations of Scripture that are based on the English translation of the Bible. When you go back and study the original language of the Scriptures, you will find error in all denominational teachings. That's why each religious group separates themselves, and that should tell us something is wrong. I'm just trying to get you to understand that it's all about Jesus, and enjoy Jesus, and do not worship what man calls "church."

We can gather together in our homes; we can gather

together in a garage; it doesn't matter, the fact remains, that we must gather together. Why? Because people need people, and God lives in people. Although we all have our faults, and we all have our little personalities, and sometimes we are not what we are supposed to be, but we are the church, God's chosen people, and we must love each other. If we had walked in some of those people's shoes, we would need somebody to help us as well. It's not our job to go around policing everybody, and judging others; it's our job to represent Christ and do what He would do.

We need to enjoy Jesus as we gather to learn the Scriptures together, as we praise the Lord together, and as we learn how to pray for each other. It's enjoyable to see God bless His people, and to interact with His children. Maybe sometimes we don't get very much out of the services, but we should still go and try to be a blessing to others. We do not gather together to discuss sports, or business, or travels, or houses and cars, but we gather together to discuss the Lord's business. To share Jesus with others, to help those who need help, to give our monies to the poor and needy, and when we do this, God is pleased, and He blesses us with His Spirit.

When attending church becomes boring and stagnant, it's because we are not following the biblical way of worship. It should be exciting to gather with God's people and to hear a Spirit–filled sermon, and to see how God's people are growing. It should be exciting to share what God has done in our own lives. I have been in revival services around the country, when you just couldn't wait to get to church, because you knew that God was doing something, and you wanted to be in on it. The church in the first century was a community of believers, not this "big me, little you" mentality. No one is more important than the other, and God teaches us through each other.

To have a good church, there must be "spiritual organization," "sound doctrine," "godly living," and a "zeal for good works." May we all strive to be the church, and to have the right attitude when we do gather together. There should be no bickering, or jealousy, or gossiping, or loving the world and its pleasures, but focusing on pleasing the Lord, because after all, the church belongs to Him! Enjoy Jesus in His church, and He will bless you more than you ever thought possible.

Enjoy Jesus Through Suffering

My brethren, count it all joy when ye fall into divers
temptations.

—James 1:2

James, the half brother of our Lord, was writing to first
century Jews, who had come to faith in Messiah, and they
were being persecuted by the unbelieving Jews. They were
still meeting in the synagogues with the other Jews, and
this could be the first epistle written to the believers in the
first century. He is not telling them to rejoice just because
they are going through trials. Some people act pious when
they are going through trials, and yet they go around with
a long, sad face. But James is saying, you will not be recon-
ciled to God until you know that trials are not an end within
themselves, but God is taking you to somewhere greater in
your faith, and this is joy!

It would drive us crazy to try and always find the rea-
soning behind every problem we have. I have heard many
believers say, "Well, there is a reason for everything." But
life is filled with trials, simply because there is sin in the

world, and some trials and circumstances are past finding out. But we know that if we love Jesus, that He will turn that trial into a blessing if we stay faithful to Him.

The Bible tells us in Psalm 73 that even the wicked may prosper and live to be old, and the righteous may suffer. But we are to be mature enough in our Savior to know that this life is temporary, and the wicked will be punished throughout all of eternity. So what if a wicked person has more wealth than me; so what if a wicked man lives longer on earth than me; it will not count for him on judgment day. I am not supposed to measure God's blessings just by how much money I have, or how long I live on earth. I am to rejoice in Christ even through the trials of life.

The first century believers were persecuted greatly for their faith, but look what happened. Through their dedication and commitment the gospel spread throughout the entire world, and now you and I are a part of God's eternal kingdom. Rejoice in that trial you are going through, because God will make you stronger, He will teach you more faith, and He wants to take you higher than you have ever been before.

Sometimes we suffer because we make decisions: "For what glory is it, if, when ye be buffeted for your faults, ye shall take it patiently?" (1 Pet. 2:20). But God takes our bad choices in life and turns them into something glorious for Him. What about Peter? He failed Christ; He denied Him; but just look what a powerful preacher he became. Jesus knew that Peter would fail, but He also saw what he would become one day. Maybe you have failed the Lord, but rejoice because God can take your mistake and make you a strong soldier in the army of the Lord.

Sometimes we suffer because there is sin in the world, and not because we did anything to cause it. Do you remember the story of the man born blind in John 9? The disciple asked Jesus, "Master, who did sin, this man, or his parents, that he was born blind?" Jesus answered, "Neither hath this man sinned, nor his parents; but that the works of God should be made manifest in him" (John 9:2–3). That man was a good opportunity for Jesus to show forth His power and love. We should never be guilty of telling someone that they are being judged for their own sins, just because they are sick. And even though we have sorrow when we or someone we love is sick, we can rejoice knowing that God may work through that sickness for His glory. When the apostle Paul had a thorn in the flesh, God told him, "My grace is sufficient for thee; for my strength is made perfect in weakness" (2 Cor. 12:9). Paul asked the Lord three times to remove it, but God knew that Paul would be exalted out of measure if he didn't have the thorn in the flesh. As I look back on my own life, I can see where God has used my mistakes and my trials to keep me from becoming prideful or high-minded. There are those today who tell us that if we are sick it is because we do not have enough faith, but that is not always the case. And there again, we do not rejoice in the suffering as a thing of itself—no one wants to suffer—but we can rejoice knowing that the Lord loves us enough that He will bring something good out of it.

The most important kind of suffering is when we suffer for Jesus, when we take up our cross and follow Him, when people ridicule us, and make fun of us, because we are serving Jesus. We certainly need to rejoice when the world rejects us because we are believers in Jesus. There is coming a great day for all believers who suffered for His name. The apostles suffered, and most of them died for preaching the gospel, and the Bible tell us that the twelve foundations of the New Jerusalem will be named after the twelve disciples. They will have great rewards in Heaven one day, as everyone will who suffered for their faith. "If so be that we suffer with him, that we may be also glorified together" (Rom. 8:17b). "If we suffer, we shall also reign with him" (2 Tim.2:12).

God has chosen us worthy to suffer for Him, and we should rejoice. This idea that everything is going to work out in this life, and everybody is going to love us, is not found in the Scriptures. Jesus said, "If the world hate you, ye know that it hated me before it hated you" (John 15:18).

To show us that suffering can lead to rejoicing, just think about Jesus our Lord. He suffered willingly, and He suffered from His own family, and His own people. He was despised and rejected, and finally was nailed to a cross, and He was the perfect, sinless Lamb of God! That suffering of Jesus, which seems so unfair and so cruel, has brought salvation to the world. We can rejoice today because Christ suffered in our place. So maybe we can look at suffering from God's perspective, and see His grace and mercy through it all.

Enjoy Jesus in the Holy Land

One of the greatest ways to enjoy Jesus, is to take a pilgrimage to Israel. Years ago, it made a huge impact on my life, and each year I can hardly wait to walk in the footsteps of my Lord. We spend so much time and money on things that do not help our spiritual life, and just one trip to Israel can make Jesus more real to you, and increase your knowledge of the Bible more than going to any Bible college. My youngest son has gone to Israel with me twice, and I can definitely see a big change in his life. He is more concerned about spiritual things, and more interested in other people coming to know Christ. It is the greatest gift you can ever give to your children.

To view the golden city of Jerusalem from the Mount of Olives is a sight that every Christian should see. When you walk in the old city of Jerusalem, you get somewhat of the same feeling as it would have been when Jesus carried His cross through town passing by all of the vendors and markets. Walking down the Mount of Olives, where Jesus came riding on a donkey, and the people were shouting, "Hosanna, Blessed is the King of Israel that cometh in the name of the Lord," is an experience you will never forget. To pray in the Garden of Gethsemane will give you a greater understanding of the agony Jesus suffered, and where He was in relation to the city when they arrested Him. Just to go to the Garden Tomb and reflect on the crucifixion, and the resurrection, will make an everlasting impression on your life, just to know that your sins were paid for, and if Jesus had not risen, there would be no hope for any of us.

As you leave Jerusalem, and travel some thirty–five hundred feet down through the gorges, and through the desert, you can get a better understanding of what Jesus meant when He said, "We must go up to Jerusalem," and how walking from Jerusalem back up to Galilee was a very hard journey. When you reach the lowest point on earth, the Dead Sea, you enter into the Judean wilderness, where John the Baptist preached, and you can see what a godly man he must have been to draw people from everywhere, to the middle of nowhere to hear his message of, "Repent ye, for the kingdom of Heaven is at hand!" To realize that John was such a powerful figure that he baptized the Messiah of Israel in the muddy Jordan.

As you travel up the Jordan valley, you can see the Samaritan mountains on the west and the mountains of Gilead on the east. Many Old Testament stories come to life as we stop at places like Beth Shean and see the ruins of a Roman theater that shows you how people lived in the first century. Driving closer to the Sea of Galilee, your heart will beat faster and faster knowing that you are going to stay on the shore of Galilee and see where Jesus of Nazareth had His public ministry. The first night there, you can hardly sleep, knowing the next morning you may see Capernaum, or Chorazin, or the Mount of Beatitudes, or ride a boat across the Sea of Galilee and see the very same mountains that Jesus saw. While you stand on the top of Mount Arbel and overlook the Plain of Gennesaret, you can see the entire Galilee area where people came from everywhere to hear and see this man called Jesus! All of His miracles come to your mind, especially the feeding of the multitude, and Sermon on the Mount, and the miracles He performed out on the sea. I have had the wonderful privilege of baptizing hundreds of people in the Jordan River, and seeing many of them make true commitments to Christ, and their lives were changed before my very eyes.

To get a geographical picture of the gospel accounts will change the way you read the Bible, following Jesus across the receding hillsides. To just think, "Here I am, in the very same place where Jesus walked." The stories that have brought solace and comfort to millions throughout the centuries bring on new meaning when you are actually there where it all took place. To smell the land, the feel of the air, to see the culture, to taste of the food, will help to put you in the everyday lifestyles of people in Jesus' time.

Journeying northward to Caesarea Philippi you can see the mountains and valleys that Jesus traveled with His disciples. When you go to places like Cana and Nazareth, you can see what humble beginnings Jesus grew up in, and how

He must have looked over the hill and saw the Jezreel Valley many times, where so many battles took place in the history of Israel, knowing that one day He would return to the earth, when all of the nations will come against Israel in the last days. As you drive through the valley, you can see Mount Carmel, where Elijah slew the prophets of Baal. Traveling southward to the ancient city of Caesarea, that was built in 22 B.C. by Herod the Great, you can see an example of the splendor of the Roman world, and this is the place where the gospel was first preached officially to the Gentiles. When Peter preached to Cornelius, and where the apostle Paul was sent from that very seaport to Rome, where the gospel then spread into the known world. And there you are, two thousand years later, standing where it all begin.

You realize how indebted we are to the Jewish people, and to the nation of Israel, for giving us the Bible, for giving us the Messiah, who not only loves the Jews, but has included us Gentiles in His kingdom!

Just an average amount of money, and just a few days of your life, can change the way you look at Jesus and the Bible. Do it my friend, and enjoy Jesus in a richer, deeper way!

You learn to have a love for Israel, and how to properly interpret the Scriptures. We are supposed to be praying for the "peace of Jerusalem" (Ps. 122:6). This is missing in the average Gentile church today. Why should we pray for the peace of Jerusalem?

1. **Because God said He would bless those who support Israel!** (Gen. 12:3; Ps. 122:6). God has promised to bless those who support Israel, and those who pray for the peace of Jerusalem, that's just the way it is folks.

2. **Because we are indebted to the Jewish people.** "Who are Israelites; to whom pertaineth the adoption, and the glory, and the covenants, and the giving of the law, and the service of God, and the promises; Whose are the fathers, and of whom as concerning the flesh Christ [Messiah] came, who is over all, God blessed for ever. Amen" (Rom. 9:4–5). The main reason we are indebted to the Jews, is because the Messiah, the Lord Jesus Christ, came to the world through Israel.

3. **Because the Jews have to be saved like the Gentiles.** "Brethren, my heart's desire and prayer to God for Israel is, that they might be saved" (Rom. 10:1). Jesus told a very religious Jew, Nicodemus, that he "must be born again" (John 3:3). We need to pray for Israel, because they are not saved by trying to keep the law; they must accept *Yeshua* (Jesus) as their Messiah to be saved.

4. **Because of the priority God has given.** "For I am not ashamed of the gospel of Christ; for it is the power of God unto salvation to every one that believeth; to the Jew first, and also to the Greek" (Rom. 1:16). Not it "was," but it "is" the power of God unto salvation to every one that believeth. This is the pattern that we are to follow. The greatest thing a church or individual can do is go by

God's pattern. Most churches have missionaries all over the world, but they place Israel on the back burner. Of course we need to preach the gospel to all the world, but it is supposed to begin with Israel. If you want your life to be blessed, support ministries who carry the gospel to the unbelieving Jews. When you look at the book of Acts, this is the way the disciples carried the gospel of Messiah: they went to Jerusalem first (Acts 2), then to Samaria (Acts 8), then to the Gentiles (Acts 10). When you read about the apostle Paul, who was called by God, to carry the gospel to the Gentiles, where did he go first when he entered into the Gentile cities? He went to the Jewish synagogues first, because this was the mandate God had given him. We need to get back to the priority God has laid down in the Bible.

5. **Because Israel is partially blinded.** "For I would not, brethren, that ye should be ignorant of this mystery, lest ye should be wise in your own conceits; that blindness in part is happened to Israel, until the fulness of the Gentiles be come in" (Rom. 11:25). We need to pray for Israel that God will remove the blindness, that they will see their need of their Messiah. It is through their unbelief that we had a chance to be saved, and we must not have anti-Semitic feelings toward God's people (Rom. 11:13-36).

When someone goes to the Holy Land, their eyes are also opened to the things that we have been missing. We know enough to get to Heaven, but we Gentiles need to rightly divide the Word of truth so God will bless us with His Spirit.

Enjoy Jesus in Death

Some may wonder how a person can enjoy death. Well, a person cannot enjoy death unless they know the one who conquered death, The Lord Jesus Christ! This was the reason Jesus came into the world.

> Forasmuch then as the children are partakers of flesh and blood, he also himself likewise took part of the same; that through death he might destroy him that had the power of death, that is, the devil; And deliver them who through fear of death were all their lifetime subject to bondage.
>
> —Hebrews 2:14–15

Just as Aaron's rod became a serpent and swallowed up Pharoah's magician's serpents, death was swallowed up in the death of the Messiah (Exod. 7:10–13; 1 Cor. 15:54). Through dying, Jesus gained the victory over death, because death could not hold the giver of life. "He tasted death for every man" (Heb. 2:9).

Even in the Old Testament we find words like this: "Precious in the sight of the Lord is the death of his saints" (Ps. 116:15). The Old Testament saints, who trusted in God, who believed in the coming Messiah, they too, were set free from the fear of death.

When we come to the New Testament, we find numerous verses that give us the assurance that physical death is only a departure from earth, and an arrival in the presence of Christ. "For to me to live is Christ, and to die is gain. . . . For I am in a strait betwixt two, having a desire to depart, and to be with Christ; which is far better" (Phil. 1:21,23).

The disciples, as well as the apostle Paul, knew beyond a shadow of a doubt, that Christ had risen, and that death was nothing to be afraid of. That is how they could stare physical death in the face. "We are confident, I say, and willing rather to be absent from the body, and to be present with the Lord" (2 Cor. 5:8). Notice the wording, "confident," "willing rather"—does that sound like someone who is afraid to die? We will never accomplish much for God's kingdom in this life until we are confident of the next life.

One of the great passages in the words of Jesus is recorded in, John 14:1–3, "Let not your heart be troubled: ye believe in God, believe also in me. In my Father's house are many mansions: if it were not so, I would have told you. I go to prepare a place for you. And if I go and prepare a place for you, I will come again, and receive you unto myself; **that where I am, there ye may be also.**" Jesus was comforting His disciples just before He went to the cross, and that has become one of the favorite passages of Scripture for many saints down through the years. It was my father's favorite, who just went to be with the Lord this past year. I remember sitting by his bedside and reading those verses, and they brought such comfort and joy to his heart. But notice that the ultimate design of Jesus coming into the world, dying on the cross, and rising again, is for us to be where He is! "Where I am, there ye may be also." The only way that we can be where Jesus is, is to die physically. Sin came into the world, and the wages of sin is death (Rom. 6:23). But even though that be true, Jesus the Christ has reversed it. "I am the resurrection, and the life: he that believeth in me, though he were dead, yet shall he live" (John 11:25). So we can have joy in knowing that God has promised us life eternal through faith in His Son Jesus Christ. Even though we will die physically, Jesus says we will live again.

I think many professing believers say they believe in life everlasting, but they somehow never apply it to their lives, and they live in unbelief. We spend all the money we can rake up in order to save our physical life, and we worry about having enough insurance to cover the doctor bills, but we spend little time and effort drawing close enough to Christ to let Him take the fear of death away.

We may live to be old, but sooner or later we have to die; that is one thing, we will have to die. "And as it is appointed unto men once to die, but after this the judgment" (Heb. 9:27). All of the great saints in the Bible had to die, except Enoch and Elijah. Even Jesus had to die! God does not want us to live our lives in fear, but in the assurance that we will be with Him when we leave this world.

We can enjoy the fact that when that day comes to us, we will leave this world of sin and sorrow, and be in the presence of the one who died for us on the cross and rose again. I have seen many people draw their last breath on earth, and to those whose bodies were beaten up with pain, it was a release. I believe God will give us dying grace, and we will go into another spiritual dimension, and we will long to be with Jesus. That is why we need to be enjoying Jesus now, so when death comes, it will be the greatest day of our life. The closer we live to Him now, the more enjoyable death will be.

There is a place we go to in Jerusalem each year, a dungeon, in what many scholars believe to be the house of Caiaphas. They believe that Jesus spent the night in this dungeon, and there are carved Christian markings in the dungeon that date back to the fourth or fifth century. Scholars believe Jesus was questioned and beaten there before being led away to Pontius Pilate the next morning (Matt. 27:1–2). We gather our group close to each other in that dark, musty dungeon, and we sing:

When I come to the river at ending of day
When the last winds of sorrow have blown
They'll be somebody waiting to show me the way
I won't have to cross Jordan alone
I won't have to cross Jordan alone
Jesus died all my sins to atone

When the darkness I see

He'll be waiting for me

I won't have to cross Jordan alone

Enjoy Jesus in the Messianic Kingdom

> . . . and they lived and reigned with Christ a thousand years.
>
> —Revelation 20:4b

> . . . and shall reign with him a thousand years.
>
> —Revelation 20:6b

While these verses give us the period of time (one thousand years) for the millennium reign of Messiah, the belief in a messianic kingdom does not rest on these verses alone. There is a massive amount of material concerning the messianic kingdom. There are well over a hundred verses in the Old Testament alone. While the Old Testament prophets clearly saw a period of time of peace on the earth in the future, they did not know when or how long that time would last.

There are four unconditional, unfulfilled covenants that God made with Israel. God keeps His promises, so these four covenants must be fulfilled, and they must be fulfilled in the future. They can only be fulfilled within the framework of a messianic kingdom.

1. **The Abrahamic Covenant**—This covenant says that the seed of Abraham will develop into a nation that will possess the land of Israel with definite borders. While there still exists a nation called Israel today, they have never possessed all of the promised land in their history. For this covenant to be fulfilled, there must be a future Kingdom age. God also promised this to Abraham, personally, as well as, Isaac and Jacob. There must be a messianic kingdom for this to happen.

2. **The Palestinian Covenant**—This covenant speaks of a regathering of the Jews to the land of Israel after their dispersion. The dispersion has already happened, and is still going on today, but the regathering has also started. Less than twenty–five years ago, five hundred thousand Jews were living in the land of Israel; now there are over six million. But this is only a prefigure of the real gathering, and the only way that all of the Jews can be in the land of Israel requires a future kingdom.

3. **The Davidic Covenant**—God promised David that from his seed there would be an eternal dynasty, an eternal throne, an eternal kingdom, and one eternal person. The only way for that to happen is for the person to be eternal—Jesus the Messiah! The angel told Mary in Luke 1:32, "He shall be great, and shall be called the Son of the Highest; and the Lord God shall give unto

him the throne of is father David." The reestablishment of David's throne and the Messiah's rule still awaits a future fulfillment. It requires a messianic kingdom.

4. **The New Covenant**—"Behold the days come, saith the Lord, that I will make a new covenant with the house of Israel, and with the house of Judah; Not according to the covenant that I made with their fathers in the day that I took them by the hand to bring them out of the land of Egypt; which my covenant they brake, although I was an husband unto them, saith the Lord; But this shall be the covenant that I will make with the house of Israel; After those days, saith the Lord, I will put my law in their inward parts, and write it in their hearts; and will be their God, and they shall be my people. And they shall teach no more every man his neighbor, and every man his brother, saying, Know the Lord; for they shall all know me, from the least of them unto the greatest of them, saith the Lord; for I will forgive their iniquity, and I will remember their sin no more. Thus saith the Lord, which giveth the sun for a light by day, and the ordinances of the moon and of the stars for a light by night, which divideth the sea when the waves thereof roar; The Lord of hosts is his name. If those ordinances depart from before me, saith the Lord, then the seed of Israel also shall cease from being a nation for ever. Thus saith the Lord, If Heaven above can be measured, and the foundations of the earth searched out beneath, I will also cast off all the seed of Israel for all that they

have done, saith the Lord" (Jer. 31:31–37). This covenant will supersede the Mosaic covenant, because God's law will be on their hearts, not on tablets of stone. The old covenant required the blood of animals, but the new covenant required the blood of the Messiah, Jesus. The old covenant was by works, the new covenant is by faith. The New Covenant has already started (Matt. 26:28), but will not be fulfilled completely, until all Israel is saved (Rom. 11:26)—not every Jew that has been born, but those who are alive when the Messiah sets up His kingdom. There must be a messianic kingdom for this to happen.

Jesus spoke of the messianic kingdom in Matthew 19:28:

Verily I say unto you, That ye which have followed me, in the regeneration when the Son of man shall sit in the throne of his glory, ye shall also sit upon the twelve thrones, judging the twelve tribes of Israel.

And I appoint unto you a kingdom, as my Father hath appointed unto me; That ye may eat and drink at my table in my kingdom, and sit on thrones judging the twelve tribes of Israel.

—Luke 22:29–30

There are more passages concerning this future kingdom than we have space to write, but read these passages:

Psalm 15:1–5; Psalm 24:1–6; Isaiah 2:2–4; Isaiah 11:6–9; Isaiah 65:17–25; Micah 4:1–5; Zechariah 14:9; and Ezekiel 47:1–12. You will find that those who are living in that thousand–year reign of Christ will be living in a universal peace. The Lord will reign from Jerusalem, and His Word will stop all warfare. There will be peace in the animal kingdom, and the glory of God will permeate the entire world. The Dead Sea will even have fish for the first time in history, as the millennial river will run from the Mediterranean Sea to the Dead Sea.

Satan will be bound, and it will be a time of prosperity like never in the history of the world. This kingdom will be characterized by truth, holiness, and righteousness. People will enjoy the fruits of their labors. Man will be at peace with man, and man will be at peace with the animals. You may have heard the old gospel song, "Peace in the Valley"— well, the lion will lay down with the lamb, just like the song says.

That is one reason why we need to be living for Jesus here and now, and doing what we can for His kingdom. Our place in that messianic kingdom will be determined on how we have served Christ in this life. Every time I travel to Israel, there is something in my spirit that tells me that one day I will be a part of that wonderful reign of Christ, when he shall rule and reign from Jerusalem, and we will go up to Jerusalem each year to celebrate the Feast of Tabernacles (Zech. 14:16).

Enjoy Jesus in Heaven

After the thousand–year reign of Christ will begin the eternal order. The place is described in Revelation 21–22. Let me just quickly mention a few things the Bible says will not be in Heaven, and then a few things that will be in Heaven:

* * * * *

1. No crying, no sorrow, no death, no pain
2. No sin, no unbelievers
3. No sun, no moon, no night
4. No temple
5. No curse

* * * * *

1. The glory of God
2. All saints of God
3. A city fifteen hundred miles foursquare, fifteen hundred miles high, made of pure gold, with jasper walls, gates of pearl, and multicolored foundations
4. The tree of life
5. A pure river, crystal clear

»

And, **THE LORD GOD ALMIGHTY**! He will be there, and we shall see His face. I've told people before, that it wouldn't matter what Heaven looked like, as long as Jesus was there. But not only will we see Jesus, we will live in that city that He has prepared for His children. Folks, if there were no Heaven, we might as well just eat, drink, and be merry, and forget it all (1 Cor. 15:32). But the Scriptures tell us that it is impossible for God to lie (Titus 1:2), and He has promised us a place when all of life's troubles are over. If there were no Heaven, there would be no need to preach another sermon, or sing another song. Heaven is real, and all of the saved people will be there one day.

The great plan of God is for His children to live with Him forever! We were created for His pleasure (Rev. 4:11). We have the stamp of God on all of us, but if we accept His Son and our personal Savior, then we will get to enjoy Jesus throughout all of eternity.

There have been times when I thought, if I had only been there when Jesus walked the shores of Galilee, and if I only could have heard those beautiful parables, and if I could have seen those supernatural miracles, and if I could have just seen His face like those people did in the first century. But then it comes to me, I will hear Him, and I will see Him, but when I do, He will be in all of His glory, and Abraham will be there, and Moses, and Joshua, and David, and all of the Old Testament saints. All of Jesus' disciples will there, Paul will be there, and all of the saints who have ever lived. My earthly father, who left us this past year, will be there. If you have been born again, even if we never meet in this life, we will meet in Heaven.

O yes, enjoying Jesus will be the greatest part of Heaven, and we need to start enjoying Him now!